VIRGINIA COLONIAL ABSTRACTS

Vol. XXIV
York County
1633 - 1646

Abstracted by
Beverley Fleet

This volume was reproduced from
an 1961 edition located in the
publishers private library,
Greenville, South Carolina

Please direct all Correspondence & Orders to:

Southern Historical Press, Inc.
P.O. Box 1267
375 W Broad Street
Greenville, S.C. 29602-1267

Originally published: Richmond, VA 1961
Reprinted: Southern Historical Press, Inc.
ISBN: 978-0-89308-515-5
Printed in the United States of America

SUBJECT INDEX

PREFACE

In the York records mist prevails. It has prevailed for 300 years with no signs of the clouds clearing. If anyone thinks he can give a final answer in interpretation he is an ass. That's all.

It is this. The originals are written in such a manner that they can be read in various ways. And they have been - to our confusion.

1st. The earliest book, 1633 plus with skipping dates, is evidently a 17th century transcript of an original now lost. This transcript being of selected items, some plainly in error. Yet this, perforce, must be accepted as the first York record. The most unfortunate mistake being in the name of Capt. Nicholas Martiau, which gives rise to the uncomfortable thought that error may apply, or almost certainly does apply, to other names appearing in these abstracts.

2nd. In regard to the handwriting. It is difficult to distinguish between the capital F and the capital H. Fellgate or Hellgat are as you please. The capitals K, L and R are similar. Almost any entry appearing in these abstracts as Lee, particularly in the case of Richd. Lee, may much more easily be read as Kee. Incidentally Henry Lee always appears as Lee and plainly se. The small u, v and n are identical. The small g is always left wide open at the top so appears a better y than the y itself. The small letters c, i, j, m, n, r, u, v, w, are usually run together, so in any combination are to be guessed at only.

Transcripts of the early York records were made in 1894. While not altogether to be relied upon, they prove a great time saver, and give a different point of view in interpretation. I have worked with them constantly at hand and would advise that anyone else working in the originals avail themselves of this assistance - but not too much.

York was a port of entry. Many records of persons from other sections are here. The late Morgan Poitiaux Robinson told me these records were the most valuable now existing in Virginia. He knew.

These abstracts will be subject to many corrections. Right or wrong, it is my intention to carry forward a second and third volume of York abstracts. As far as 1652 if possible.

                                                    Beverley Fleet

30th April 1945.

YORK COUNTY CHART

Charles River
1634 - 1642/3

York
1642/3 - 1945 plus

* * * * * * * * * * * * * * * * * * * *

Gloucester
1651 - 1945 plus

New Kent
1654 - 1945 plus

* * * * * * * * * * * * * * * * * * *

King and Queen
1691 - 1945 plus

King William
1702 - 1945 plus

Hanover
1721 - 1945 plus

Louisa
1742 - 1945 plus

Matthews
1791 - 1945 plus

See Virginia Counties. Morgan Poitiaux Robinson. Page 65. Chart 3
Bulletin Virginia State Library. Vol.9. 1916.

York County Records

The following are available in the Archives Division of the Virginia
State Library, Richmond, Virginia.

No.1	Deeds, Orders, Wills, etc.	1635 - 1657	and	1691 - 1694
No.2	Orders, Wills, etc.	1645 - 1649		
No.3	Deeds, Orders, Wills, etc.	1657 - 1662		
No.4	" " " "	1664 - 1672		
No.5	" " " "	1672 - 1676		
	" " " "	1675 - 1684	Transcript	
No.7	" " " "	1684 - 1687		
No.8	" " " "	1687 - 1691		
	" " " "	1690 - 1694	Transcript	
	" " " "	1694 - 1697	"	
	" " " "	1697 - 1702	"	
	Deeds	1691 - 1701	"	

Also:
Stanard's Mss. Notes. 2 volumes.

York County
Deeds, Orders, Wills, etc.NO. 1
1633 - 1657
1691 - 1694

Items 1691 - 1694 will be omitted from this, Vol.24, Virginia Colonial
Abstracts. Also the records from 1652 on. Volume 2 of the York County
begins 1645. It seemed best to continue these abstracts according to
date.

This volume No.1 Of the York County records is unquestionably a transcript of certain items from an original now lost. It was made during
the colonial period. The outstanding error in this transcript is in
the spelling of the name of Capt. Nicholas Martiau, which is shown as
Capt. Nicholas Martian throughout No.1. After a considerable amount
of wrangling on the part of modern historians the spelling 'Martian'
was finally decided to be in error.

No.1 - No entries of any value until page 4.

No.1. p.4
        Att a Court held att Utimaria the 12th of July 1633
Present   Capt John Utie   Mr Wm English
                Capt Nicholas Martian   Mr Lyonell Rowlston
                Capt Robert Follgate   Richard Townsene

No.1. p.5
        A Court at Utimaria 12 August 1633
Present   Capt John Utie   Mr Wm English
                Capt Nicholas Martian   Mr Lyonell Rowlston
                Capt Robert Fellgate   Richard Townsene

No.1. p.6
        A Court at Utimaria 20 Sept 1633
Present   Capt Wm Clayborne   Mr Wm English
                Capt John Utie   Mr Lyonell Rowlston
                Capt Nicholas Martian   Mr Richard Townshene
                Cap't Robert Felgate

No.1. p.7
        A Court at Utimaria 5 Oct 1633
Present   Capt John Utie   Mr Wm English
           Capt Nicholas Martian   Mr Lyonell Rowlston
           Capt Robt Fellgate

No.1. p.8
        A Court at York 7 Jan. 1633/4
Present   Capt John Utie   Mr Lyonell Rowlston
           Capt Nicholas Martian   Mr Richard Townshend
           Mr. Wm English

No.1. p.9
        A Court at Utimaria 8 April 1634
Present   Capt John West   Mr Will: English
           Capt John Utie   Mr John Chew
           Capt Nicholas Martian   Lef't: John Cheesman
           Capt Robt Fellgate

No.1 p.10
        A Court at Utimaria 5 May 1634
Present   Capt John West   Mr Wm English
           Capt John Utie   Mr John Chew
           Capt Nicholas Martian   Lef't John Cheesman

No.1. p.11
        A Court at York 7 July 1634
Present   Capt John Utie   Mr William English
           Capt Nicholas Martian   Mr John Chew
           Capt Robt Felgate

No.1. p.12
        A Court at Utimaria 12 Aug 1634
Present   Capt John West   Mr Wm English
           Capt John Utie
           Capt Robt Felgate

Note: The name appearing here as Martian is actually Martiau. B.F.

No.1. p.13
        A Court at Utimaria 3 Nov 1634
Present   Capt John West   Capt Robt Felgate
           Capt John Utie   Mr John Chew
           Capt Nicholas Martian

No.1. p.13.   Whereas Thomas Trotter was seated on 50 acres, found to
be within the dividend of Serj't John Wayne, Wayne now deeds the land
to him in consideration of 50 acres he shall choose elsewhere. Dated
4th Sept. 1633. Signatures not shown. Wit. by Will Clayborne and John
Utie.

No.1. p.14
        A Court held at Utimaria 13 Jan 1634/5.
Present   Capt John West   Mr Wm English
           Capt John Utie   Mr John Chew
           Capt Nicholas Martian

No.1. p.14.   Wm Pryor assigns Capt John Utie all interest in a house
and land adjoining "the plantation of Broche westward and to the Creek
southward".

No.1. p.15
        A Court held at - , 13 April 1635
Present   Capt John West   Capt Nicholas Martian
           Capt John Utie   Mr John Chew
           Capt Robt Fellgate   Leif't John Cheesman

No.1. p.16
        A Court at York 15 June 1635
Present   Capt John Utie   Mr Will English
           Capt Robt Fellgate   Mr John Chew
           Capt Nicholas Martian

No.1. p.17
        A Court held at York 13 July 1635
Present   Capt John Utie   Mr Will English
           Capt Robt Fellgate   Mr John Chew
           Capt Nicholas Martian   Lef't John Cheesman

No.1. p.18
        A Court at Mr John - , 2 Nov 1635
Present   Capt John Utie   Mr Wm English
           Capt Nicholas Martian   Mr John Chew
           Capt Robt Felgate

No.1. p.19
        A Court at Leift John Cheesmans
Present   Capt John Utie   Mr John Chew
           Capt Nicholas Martian   Mr Richard Townshend
           Capt Robt Fellgate   Lef't John Cheesman

No.1. p.20
        A Court at Utimaria 18 Jan 1635/6
Present   Capt John Utie   Mr Richard Townshend
           Capt Nicholas Martian   Lef't John Cheeseman
           Capt Robt Fellgate

No.1. p.21
        A Court at Utimaria 12 Feb 1635/6
Present   Capt John West Esq'r Governour etc
           Capt John Utie   Mr John Chew
           Capt Nicholas Martian   Mr Richard Townshend
                                       Lef't John Cheesman

No.1. p.22
        A Court "att Mr John Chew his house in Charles River", 24th
        March 1635/6.
Present   Capt John Utie   Mr Richard Townshend
           Capt John Chew   Lef't John Cheeseman

No.1. p.23
        A Court at Capt Nicholas Martian 28 April 1636
Present   Capt John West Esq'r Governour etc
           Capt John Utie Esqr   Mr John Chew
           Capt Robt Fellgate   Mr Rich'd Townshend

Note: The record of the Court of 28th April 1636 indicated that Capt.
John Utie was at this time a member of the Council.   B.F.

No.1. p.24
          A Court at Mr Richard Townshend's house in Charles River.
          30th June 1636.
Present   Capt John West Esqr Governour etc
          Capt Nicholas Martian   Mr John Chew
          Capt Robt Fellgate   Mr Richd Townshends
                                    Leift John Cheeseman

No.1. p.25
          A Court at Mr Wm Pryor's house 28 July 1636
Present   Capt John West Esqr Governor etc
          Capt John Utie Esqr   Mr John Chew
          Capt Nicholas Martian   Mr Richd Townshend
                                    Left John Cheeseman

No.1. p.26
          A Court at Lef't John Cheeseman's house 18 Aug 1636
Present   Capt John West Esqr Governour etc
          Capt Nicholas Martian   Mr Richard Townshend
          Mr John Chew   Left John Cheesman

No.1. p.27
          A Court at Utamaria 21 Nov 1636
Present   Capt John West Esqr Governour etc
          Capt John Utie Esqr   Capt Robt Fellgate
          Mr George Minifie Esqr   Mr John Chew

(Note: Wm. G. Stanard's Mss. Notes, York Co. p.4. "George Minifee came
to Virginia in 1623: burgess for James City County 1629; member of the
Council 1635 - 1645". His residence "Littleton" on James River had the
finest gardens and orchards in Virginia. Said to have been the first
who introduced the peach in America.   B.F.   )

No.1. p.28
          A Court at Capt Robt Fellgate's house 12 Jan 1636/7.
Present   Capt John West Esqr Governor etc
          Capt John Utie Esq'r   Mr John Chew
          Capt Robt Fellgate   Mr Rich'd Townshend
                                    Left John Cheesman

No.1. p.29
A Court at Capt Christopher Wormelyes house 15 Feb 1636/7
Present   Sergeant Mayor George Dunn Esqr   (sic)
            Capt Christopher Wormely   Mr Wm Pryor
            Mr John Cheeseman   Mr Hugh Owen

(Note: The following from Mr. W. G. Stanard's Mss. Notes, York Co. p.5.
"George Donne was a son of the poet, and was Serjeant Major of Virginia
and member of the Council. He returned to England. See Neil".
"Capt. Christopher Wormeley was Governor of Tortuga 1632 - 1635. Came
to Virginia and was appointed member of the Council 1637 and d before
1649 leaving a son Capt Ralph Wormeley burgess and member of the
Council who settled at "Rosegill". Etc.

No.1. p.30
A Court at York 16 March 1636/7.
Present   Capt Christopher Wormeley Mr Wills Pryor
            Capt Robt Follgate   Mr Hugh Owen
            Mr John Chew
            Mr Richard Townshend

No.1. p.31
A Court at the house of Mr John Chew 25 April 1637
Present   Capt Christopher Wormeley Esqr
            Mr John Chew   Mr Richard Townshend
                                       Mr Wills Pryor

No.1. p.32
A Court at the house of Mr Richard Townshend 25 May 1637
Present   Capt Christopher Wormeley Esq
            Capt Robt Fellgate   Left John Cheesman
            Mr John Chew   Mr Will Pryor
            Mr Richard Townshend   Mr Hugh Owin

No.1. p.33 (This will is given in full)
                    "The 10th of March 1631"   (1631/2)
"In the name of God Amen This Will and Testament being the last will
and Testament of Andrew Whowell made the Tenth of March 1631 being in
his perfect senses as ever he was in his life time Wittnesseth That I
make Christopher Stookes my lawfull Overseer to see that the tenor of

The will of Andrew Whowell, 1631/2 (continued)

this my Will be performed as followeth
Imprs: First I bequeath my Soule to almighty God my maker and my body
to be buryed in the Ground and for my worldly Wealth that itt hath
pleased God to endow me with as followeth
Item: I give my brother Nathaniel Clarke one sow pig the which my
father doth owe me and one barrell of Corne when that is one and Twenty
Yeares of Age and two Henns presently and one
Item I give unto my Sister Bettris Clark Three barrells of Indian
Corne and one Pullett and one Sow.
Item I give unto my father Joseph Jolly one Sow pigg and one barrow
pigg
Item I give unto my Mother Margarett Jolly one barrow pigg
Item I give unto Francis Laster (or Lasler ?) one Sow pigg
Item the Three barrells of Corne that I give unto my sister Bottris
Clark is to be putt to use till she cometh to Age, and the Sow that I
give her they that keep her till that shoe cometh to age are to have
of the increase all she beare piggs and the Sow piggs to be putt to
the best use till that shee cometh to Age
Witnesse my hand the Day and Yeare first above written
                                    The mark of
Wittness   Andrew Whowell
Peter Mountague   "

No.1. p.34
          A Court at Mr William Pryor's 22 June 1637
Present   Capt Robt Felgate   Leif't John Cheesman
              Mr John Chew   Mr William Pryor
              Capt Richard Townshend   Mr Hugh Owin

No.1. p.35
              " In nomine domine Amen
I Adam Lynsey being sick in bodey but perfect in minde and memory
praysed be god doe make and ordaine this my last Will and Testament
in manner and forme following
Imprs: I give and bequeath my Soule to God my Maker and Redeemer and
my body to the earth and as concerneing my worldly Estate as followeth
Imprs: I give and bequeath to Ann the wife of John Jackson Two hundred pounds of Tobacco Moreover I bequeath to Christian Owin of -
perquoson Fower hundred pounds of Tobacco and what remaineth of my
Estate I bequeath unto my good friend Edward Mollson whom I make and
ordaine my Executor to see this my will performed and my Legacyes

(continued next page)

The will of Adam Lynsay (continued)

payd
In wittness whereof I have hereunto sett my hand and Seale this 30th of
July 1636
Sealed signed and delivered   the mark of
in the presence of   Adam x Lynsay
Wm Hookaday
Allexander Gregory

No.1. p.35
A true and perfect Inventory of all the goods of Adam Lynsey of York
late deceased taken and prised tho 21th of June 1637 by us whose names
are here underwritten

Impr.	One Cloath suite	120 lb Tobacco
It.	Two shirts 2 bands 3 handkercheifes	120
It.	Two old Wastcoats	015
It	Old Canvis Drawers	010
It	One hatt	020
It	one Flook bed and Covering	080
It	one Silver Whissle and Chaine	080
It	one Small boate	500
It	In Tobacco oweing Mr Stockton	600
It	Mr Young	400
It	Mr Charlton	200
It	Mr Jernew	020
It	Wm Freeman	050
It	Richard Heather	020
Item	Mr Hugh Owins man	036
Item	Certaine Carpenters Tooles	250
Item	one ould peece	030
Item	one bushell 1/2 Corne	045
		- - - -
	Sume is	2036

Wm Warren
the mark of
John IP Penrice

No.1. p.36
"An Inventory or List of all the Goods found belonging unto Ralph
Gerrard deceased in the house of Anthony Panton Clerck dwelling att
Cheisekiake taken by those whose names are unto written July the 24th
1637".
Includes "one bill of Robt Kingsayes for 0800". Total 1070 lb tobo.
Signed: Anthony Panton, Serjeant John x Wayne, Thomas Blease.

No.1. p.37
          A Court at the house of Capt Robt Fellgate 25 July 1637.
Present   Capt Christopher Wormely Esqr
               Capt Robt Fellgate   Capt Richd Townshend
               Mr John Chew   Mr Will: Pryor

No.1. p.38
          A Court at the house of Mr John Cheeseman 24 August 1637
Present   Capt Christopher Wormely Esqr
               Capt Robt Fellgate   Capt John Cheeseman
               Mr John Chew   Mr Wm Pryor
               Capt Richd Townshend   Mr Hugh Owin

No.1. p.39
          A Court at the house of Capt Christopher Wormely 30 Oct 1637
Present   Sr John Harvey Governour etc
               Capt Christopher Wormely Esqr   Capt Richd Townshene
               Capt Nicholas Martian   Capt John Cheeseman
               Mr John Chew   Mr Wm Pryor

No.1. p.40
          A Court at the house of Capt Richd Townshend 26 Dec 1637
Present   Capt Christopher Wormely Esqr
               Capt Nicholas Martian   Capt Richd Townshend
               Capt John Cheeseman   Mr Wm Pryor
               Mr John Chew   Mr Ralph Wormeley

No.1. p.41
          A Court at the house of Mr Wm Pryor 23 January 1637/8
Present   Capt Nicholas Martian   Mr William Pryor
               Mr John Chew   Mr Ralph Wormeley
               Capt Richd Townshend

No.1. p.42
          A Court at the house of Capt John Cheeseman 13 Feb 1637/8
Present   Capt Nicholas Martian   Mr Wm Pryor
               Mr John Chew   Mr Ralph Wormeley
               Capt John Cheeseman

No.1. p43
    A Court at the house of Mr John Chew 13 March 1637/8
Present   Capt Nicholas Martian   Mr William Pryor
          Capt John Cheeseman   Mr Ralph Wormeley
          Mr John Chew

No.1. p.44
    "A Court houlden att the Governours house the 18th of March
    1637" (1637/8).
Present   Capt Nicholas Martian   Mr Ralph Wormeley
          Mr William Pryor

No.1. p.44   "It is ordered by this Court that the Leases belonging
to the Governours Tennants be Recorded".

No.1. p.44.   Deed of Lease. 2 May 1635. Martin Becker, Merchant,
leases a parcel of land to Thos. Trotter, Thos. Jefferyes and John
Balyes, planters, in York in Virginia, for 11 years at 50 lb tobo
and "one fatt hogg of a yeare old" per year, payable 20th Dec. The
land "Being in the Plantation called York from the River side unto
a marked Poplrin in the woods and bounding on Mr Johnsons Land to
the Southeast on the one side and on the land of Owin Dawson on the
North west side".
Wit: Signed   Martin Becker
Charles Babb
Richd Hamlin

No.1. p.45.   Deed of Lease. 23 Oct 1636. Martin Becker, Merchant,
leases to John Penrise "of York in the Country of Virginia", 100
acres, for 9 years at 200 lb tobo per year payable 20th Dec. The
land "in the Plantation called York beginning on the head of the
Mill Swamp being the outside of his land runing back into the woods".
Wit: Signed   Martin Becker
John Hampton
Wm Hocaday

No.1. p.45.   Deed of Lease. 18 Feb 1633/4. Lyonell Rowlston to John
Balyes and Andrew Kirby of Virginia, planters, for 12 years. Yearly
rent "one Couple of Capons". A parcel of land adj the water side and
the land of Francis Compton.
Wit: Signed   Lyonell Rowlston
Thomas Burbay
Wm Torkeesent

No.1. p.46.   15th November 1632. Agreement between Lyonell Rowlston
gent and Edward Johnson. Rowlston to let Johnson a tract of land during
the life of John Johnson, his wife and Luke Johnson. The yearly rent
being "one barrow hogg of a yeare old att the Feast day of St Thomas".
If the Johnsons leave, or sell, their life interest, Rowlston to have
first refusal and they to leave it with "a Tennantable house upon itt".
The land adjoins "Will: Warren to a marked Tree by the Riverside and
soe extending backwards into the woods to the head of a Swamp".
Wit: Signed   Lyonell Rowlston
John Penrice   Edward Johnson

No.1. p.46.   Deed of Lease. 13 March 1633/4. Martin Becker "of
Plimouth within the Kingdome of England Merchant" lets to William
Warren of York in Virginia, planter, a parcel of land, during the
life of said William Warren and Ann his now wife. Yearly rent "a
good fatt hogg of the Age of one yeare old". The land "lying upon
Charles River North and upon the lands of Edmond Johnson west and
upon the land of John Jackson south and joyneing to the lands of
the said Martin Becker East".
Wit: Signed   Martin Becker
Robt Paine (This name actually
illegible. It may be Caine, or
else ?)
Francis Arkistall

No.1. p.47
        A Court at Capt Wormeleye's house in Charles County 17th
        April 1638.
Present   Capt Nicholas Martian)   Mr Wm Pryor   )
           Capt John Cheeseman   )   Mr Ralph Wormeley) Gents
           Capt Richd Townshene)

No.1. p.48
        A Court at the house of Capt Nicholas Martian in Charles
        County. 12 June 1638
Present   Capt Christopher Wormely Esqr
           Capt Nicholas Martian)
           Capt Richd Townshend   )   Gent
           Mr Wm Pryor   )
           Mr Ralph Wormeley   )

Note: We must not forget that the name Martian as shown in this early
transcript is actually Martiau.   B.F.

No.1. p.49.

A Court at Mr William Pryor's 20th July 1638.
Present   Capt William Brocas Esqr
           Capt Nicholas Martian)
           Capt John Chisman   )
           Mr John Chew   )   Gen'ts
           Capt Rich'd Townshend)
           Mr William Pryor   )

Note: There is, or rather we should say in the year 1945, that there
was in 1914, in the Royal Collection at the Hague, a portrait of Robert
Cheseman, Falconer to Henry VIII. This, painted by Hans Holbein the
Younger during his second visit to England in 1533, is (or was) one
of the world's great portraits. A photograph is before me now. It shows
the courtier in full power of manhood, aged 28. His features are high
bred, strong, kindly. The hair curled just before it reaches the collar.
The costume·simple which was customary for English gentlemen in com-
parison with the elaborate and costly outfits of the merchants of the
period. It would be impossible for me to attempt to trace the exact
relationship with Capt. John Cheeseman of York County. The family was
of Kent in England - the background of so many early Virginians. B.F.

No.1. p.50.   Deed. 20 Nov. 1635. John Utie of Utimaria Esqr sells
Edward Moulson, Sawyer, 100 acres between the land of Francis Morgan
and Mr William Pryor. Payment being 1000 ft "Sawen Boards" already
received and 800 ft more to be paid between this and 1st of March.
Wit: Signed   John Utie
Edward Major   Edward Moulson
James Besouth
Moulson assigns his interest in above 100 acres to Francis Morgan.
Dated the last day of October 1637.
Wit: Signed   Edward Moulsome
Richard Benmimge

No.1. p.50.   Will of Joseph Ham. Dated 3 March 1637/8. Probated 10th
July 1638 in Charles River Co.
Sick in body. To wife Mary Ham all land. To "my sonn and Daughter in
law John Pead and Catherine Pead" 30 young kids in full of their
legacy left them by their father deceased, John Pead. The cattle to
be in charge of wife Mary until the children be of full age to enjoy
them. To wife Mary 21 old goats. If she marry before the children are
21 the goats to be divided between them. Wife extrx.
Wit: Signed   Joseph x Ham
Robt Breckwell Minister
Pero Blan:
John Johnson   "Vera Copia Test Mar. Johnson Clk"

No.1. p.51

      Inventory of the estate of Joseph Ham of the new Poquoson,
deceased. 3 March 1638/9. Appraised by Thomas x Curtis,
Wm x Clarke and Arthur Markworth, (Inventory signed "Wm
Mackworth") of the Poquoson, planters. Sworn before Capt
John Cheeseman on 12th July 1638.

"Twenty old Goates att Two Thousand weight of Tobacco	2000
Twenty young Goates att foureteen hundred pounds	1400
One old Gote att one hundred pounds	0100
One Kid att Fifty pounds	0050
One old Feather bed and two blancketts one Rugg and	
a Boulster	0060
A parcell of ould Pewter att fifty pounds	0050
Three Iron Potts att Fo'oer score pounds	0080
One Warmeing Pann two Brass kettles one brass Bason att	0050
One Copper Kettle att Eighty pounds	0080
A parcell of old Iron ware att one hundred	0100
One old Fowleing Peice without Lock and a Shottbag	0050
One Maide Servant att seaven hundred	0700
Thirty pounds of Shott att Thirty pounds Tobacco	0030
Three payer of old Sheets 1 Doz Napkins 1 Table Cloath	0150
One Lookeing Glass att 2 pounds	0002
A parcell of old waring Cloathes fifty	0050
Two Cases Two boxes one Chest fifty pounds	0050
Three small Shoats or Swine att 1 hund and Twenty	0120
Tenn Barrells of Corne att fower hundred	0400
The Plantation for Two Yeares att five hundred	0500
	- - - -
	6552

The mark of
Thos T Cortis
The mark of
Wm x Clarke
Wm: Mackworth

         vera Copia test Mar'n Johnson   "

No.1. p.53

      A Court at the house of Capt Richd Townsend 14 Aug 1638

Present

      Capt Wm Brocas Esqr
      Capt John Cheeseman
      Capt Richard Townshend   gen't
      Mr Wm Pryor

No.1. p.54
            A Court at the house of Capt Wm Brocas Esqr 11 Sept 1638
Present   Capt Wm Brocas Esqr
            Capt Nicholas Martian) Capt Richard Townshend)
            Capt John Cheeseman   ) Mr Wm Pryor   )   gent
            Mr John Chew   )

No.1. p.55.
            A Court at the house of Capt Cheeseman 16 Oct 1638
Present   Capt Wm Brocas Esqr
            Capt Nicholas Martian) Mr John Chew)
            Capt John Cheeseman   ) Mr Wm Pryor) gent

No.1. p.56
            A Court at the house of Mr John Chew 2 Jan 1638/9.
Present   Capt Nicholas Martian) Capt Richd Townshend)
            Capt John Cheeseman   ) Mr Wm Pryor   )   gen't
            Mr John Chew   )

No.1. p.57   Deed. 1 Oct 1638. Rich'd Major of Queens Creek in Virginia,
planter, sells Thomas Bowrren (Bourne ?) of Cheiscake, cooper, 25
acres on Western side of West Creek, adjoining land of Wm Barber.
Wit: Signed Rich'd Major
Robt Booth
Rowland Burnham
"vera copia Mar. Johnson Cl Curia"

1 Oct. 1638. Thomas x Bourne assigns above 25 acres to Wm Barber of
Cheiscake, cooper,
Wit: Signed   his mark
Wm Hookeday   Tho B Bourne

No.1. p.58
            A Court at the house of Capt Nicholas Martian 12th February
            1638/9
Present   Capt Nicholas Martian   )
            Capt John Cheeseman   )   gent
            Mr John Chew   )
            Capt Richard Townshend)

No.1. p.59
        A Court at the house of Capt Richd Townshend for Charles
        River County 28th February 1638/9.
Present   Capt Wm Brocas Esqr
         Capt Nicholas Martian   (Martiau)
         Capt John Cheeseman
         Mr John Chew
         Capt Richd Townshend
         Mr Wm Pryor

No.1. p.60
        A Court at the house of Mr Wm Pryor in Charles River County,
        28th March 1639.
Present   Capt Nicholas Martian   Capt Richd Townshend
         Mr John Chew   Mr Wm Pryor

No.1. p.61
        A Court at Capt Brocas' house for Charles River County. 25th
        April 1639
Present   Sr John Harvey Knt
         Capt Wm Brocas Esqr   Capt Jno Cheeseman
         Capt Nicholas Martian   Capt Richard Townshend
         Mr John Chew   Mr Wm Pryor

No.1. p.62. Deed. 17 Jan 1638/9. John Hartwell of Charles River County,
planter, sells Tobias Freer and Robert Vause, 400 acres adj. Queens
Creek north, running along Hartwells Creek S.W. from the Saltwater,
likewise along the swamp, and also S.Sw. from the head of the swamp
to Mayden Swamp, abutting West upon both.
Wit: Signed   John x Hartwell
Tho Gybson
   his mark
Nicholas NI Jurnue

Page 63 blank.

No.1. p.64   Deed. 15 Oct 1640. William Reynolds of Chiskiake, planter,
sells Thos Denham, 200 acres in Charles River County, on Queens Creek,
bounded as by "a Pattent in my owne name beareing date the 15th day of

Deed. Reynolds to Denham (continued)

August in the yeare of our Lord God 1637".
Wit: Signed   the mark of
Wm x Smoote   Wm x Reynolds
Robt Booth
Thomas Ramsey   "vera copia Test per me
                               Robt. Booth Cl Curia "

No.1. p.65.   Deed. 28 Sept 1639. Wm Banister sells John Haukins (this
name also appears as 'John Hawkins' in this entry),   ."Fower Per-
cells of Land with the Marsh and woods runing Westward to a Creek that
lyeth North and South to the Tinkers Sheeres by the little Presim'on
Iseland".
Wit: Signed Wm Ban'ister
Tho: Larramer
Wm Smith

No.1. p.66.   Deed. 13 Nov 1639. John Utie and Robert Booth sell Thos.
Gybson 100 acres in Charles River County, at the head of a small Creek
called Queenes Creeke, running up the N side of the creek to Bryary
Swamp, including the swamp to the run of water in the swamp. All the
land from the dividend of John - (the surname here omitted from the
original record). Adjs the land of John Utie as by a survey made by
Mr Thomas Simons in 1638.
Wit: Signed   John Utie
Thomas Watts   Robert Booth
Edmund Plunckett
"Vera Copia Test per me Robt Booth Cl Curia"

John Utie and Mary his wife confirm above.
Wit: Signed   John Utie
John Baldwin   the mark of
Hugh Owin   Mary Utie: M U
Anthony Parkhurst
Thom: Lucas

No.1. p.67
         A Court held for Charles River County 27th Nov. 1640.
Present   Capt Wm Brocas Esqr Commander
           Capt Nicholas Martian   (actually Martiau)
           Mr John Chew
           Mr Hugh Owin

No.1. p.68.   Deed. 14 Nov 1640. Tho Denham of Queens Creek, planter,
sells John Vaughan, for 1000 lb tobo, 50 acres. This land bought from
Wm Reynolds 15 Oct last past, being 1/2 of 100 acres where said Thos.
Denham "now dwelleth". Refers to agreement betw Denham and 'Vaugham'
dated 2 March 1639/40
Wit: Signed   Thos Denham
Robt Booth
John Scales

No.1. p.69.   "The bounds of John Condons Land". "John Condon desyreth
a Pattent for 100 Acres of land lying in the County of Charles River".
He has 50 acres already and 50 more to be taken in a new patent which
was part of land granted to Wm Freeman about 5 years since "but to this
day there is noe body hath cleared or built uppon itt therefore John
Condon doth suppose that itt is lawfull for him to take upp for his
owne use his Pattent being voyd for want of seateing uppon itt". The
bounds according to a survey 10 Nov 1640, are adj the back Creek, North
beginning at the mouth of Gwins Creek and measuring W and by N 100
poles, etc. "If the reason should be demanded why he runs noe further
into the woods itt is this; old Attoway lives upon Cheesemans Creek
and hath his breadth double by the water syde as John Compdon doth and
if they should runn a Mile they would intercept or cutt of one the
other therefore I have taken the best course I could to prevent a
contraversie that would arrise".
"Concordat oum original".

No.1. p.70.   Deed. 12 May 1640. Joseph Jolly of new Pawquoson, planter,
sells William Clark of the new Pawquoson, planter, 350 acres formerly
granted said Jolly. Adjoins Pawquoson River, the land of said Clark
and W on the land of John Watson, etc,
Wit: Signed   Joseph x Jolly
Arthur Price
Richard Russell (signed with mark)

No.1. page 71 blank.

No.1. p.72
            A Court for Charles River County 11 Jan 1640/1. "att the
            Ordinary appointed"
Present   Capt John West Esqr   Capt Richard Townshend
              Capt Robt Fellgate   Capt John Cheeseman
              Capt Nicholas Martian   Mr Wm Pryor
              Mr John Chew   Mr Hugh Owin
                                           Mr John Baldwin

No.1. p.73
        "Att a Court held att James Citty the 18th of December
        1640: Present Sr Francis Wyatt Governour etc
        Capt John West   Capt Wm Brocas
        Mr Roger Wyngate   Mr Ambrose Harmer   "

Note:

```
                 ( George Wyatt ( Sir Francis Wyatt, Governor of
                 ( 1554 - 1624  ( Virginia, etc.
Sir Thos. Wyatt  ( m Jane Finch ( m Margaret Sandys who was a niece
  ( the Rebel )  ( (He must not  ( of Sir Edwin and of George Sandys.
  1520 - 1554    ( have had much( No descendants in Virginia.
married          ( respect for  (
   Jane Hawte    ( his father's ( Rev. Hawte Wyatt
                 ( memory when  (     1594 - 1638
                 ( he fell in   ( Minister at Jamestown.
                 ( love with her( Ancestor of the Wyatt family of
                 (              ( Virginia.
                 (
                 ( Jane Wyatt    ( Deborah Scott ( Lt. Col. Henry Fleet.
                 ( m             ( m             ( In Va. 1622.
                 ( Charles Scott ( Wm Fleet, gent.( Numerous descendants
                 ( of Edgerton   ( of Chartham   ( in Virginia.
                 (
                 ( Numerous other children
```

If anyone, however remotely descended from the Council group, has any
desire for ancestral granduer, here we are. Merely examine the pedigree
of Scott of Scots Hall, but more particularly that of Hawt. You will
find anything the heart desires from the Earl of Leicester to Lord
Guildford Dudley and Sir Philip Sidney.   B.F.

No.1. p.74. "January the 12th 1640".   (1640 - perhaps ?)
Present   Capt Jno West Esqr   Mr John Chew
          Capt Robt Fellgate   Capt Jno Cheeseman
          Capt Nicholas Martian Mr Jno Baldwin

No.1. p.75
        "Att a Quarter Court houlden att James Citty the 18th of
        September 1640"
Present   Sr Francis Wyatt Governour etc
        Capt John West   Capt Wm Brocas
        Mr Roger Wyngatt   Mr Ambrose Harmer

No.1. p.75.   Deed. 25 Dec 1640. Wm Taylor of Utimaria in Charles River
County, Virginia, merchant, sells Wm Blackley (who has already paid
Jno Utie). 100 acres in Charles River County, on Queens Creek. Adjoins
Bell Creek, beginning at Bells bridge, the line running until it meets
with "Queens house Fence", etc. This land formerly purchased from John
Utie by Taylor.
Wit: Signed   W m Taylor
Stephen x Gill
Joshua x Kinsell
Edward Phillips

No.1. p.76   River
              A Court held for Charles City County 23 March 1640/1.
Present   Capt Wm Brocas Esqr Commander
              Capt Robt Fellgate   Capt John Cheeseman
              Capt Nicholas Martian   Mr Wm Pryor
              Mr John Chew   Mr Hugh Owin
              Capt Richard Townshend

No.1. p.77
              "A Court held att James Citty the 6th of March 1640".(1640/1)
Present   Sr Francis Wyatt Knt Governour etc
              Capt John West   Mr George Minify
              Mr Wm Wingate   Capt Wm Brocas
                                          Mr Ambrose Harmer

(The name Wm Wingate appearing here is probably an error in the
original. Doubtless it should have been Roger Wingate. B.F.)

No.1. p.78
              "At a Court holden att James Citty the 5th day of March
              1640". (1640/1)
Present   Sr Francis Wyatt Knt Governour
              Capt John West   Mr George Minifey
              Capt Wm Peirce   Capt Wm Brocas
              Mr Roger Wingate   Mr Ambrose Harmer

No.1. p.78.   Will of John Jackson of Virginia, planter. Dated 22
Oct 1640. Date of probate not shown on record. Very weak in body. To
wife Ann all cleared ground within the fence. Other land for life.
She to have "my Sonn Thomas Jackson" till 21. Cattle to son Thomas.

                        (continued)

The will of John Jackson (continued)

Also to son Thomas a plantation now leased to Jeremiah Roggers.
Balance of estate to wife. 50 acres at York to be sold for benefit
of son.
Wit: Signed   his mark
Wm x Burterwood   John JI Jackson
John Shreggs

No.1. p.80. A Court for Charles River County 3 May 1640.
Present   Capt John West Esqr   Capt John Cheeseman
             Capt Wm Brocas Esq'r   Mr William Pryor
             Capt Richd Townshene

No.1. p.81
           "A Court houlden att James Citty the 20th of Aprill 1640"
Present   Sr Francis Wyatt Knt Governour
             Capt John West   Capt Tho: Willoughby
             Capt Wm Claybourne   Mr Ambrose Harmer
             Mr Rich'd Kempe   Mr Richd: Bennett
             Mr Roger Wingate

No.1. p.81.   Deed. 11 Oct 1640. Christopher Abbot of Chiskiacke in
Virginia, planter, sells Wm Sutton, 40 acres adjoining "the great
swamp" along a line of marked trees from the other swamp, etc.
Wit: Signed   Christopher Abbot
Wm Williams
   the mark of
John x Bennett

No.1. p.82.
           A Court for Charles River County "the 34th Day of May 1641"
Present   Capt John West Esqr
             Capt Wm Brocas Esq   Capt John Cheeseman
             Capt Nicholas Martian   Mr Wm Pryor

Note: Here we have a little overtime in Charles River County. The
record says the 34th of May, so I suppose it must have been.   B.F.

No.1. p.82. Deed. 21 May 1639. John Congdon "of the back Creek" in
Charles River County, planter, sells Edward Persivall of the same
place, planter, 25 acres, "upon the side of Back Creek with two

boarded houses belonging to the said Twenty five Acres of Land the one
house of Thirty foote long and the other of Twenty foote long". The
land as by patent dated 21 August 1638.
Wit: Signed   John x Congdon
Humphry Hamnar
    his mark
Peter P:R: Rigby

Note: The name Rigby as written here is a perfect example of how
carelessly this transcript was prepared.. The top of the small 'g'
was left open and the top of the small 'y' closed, so that the name
actually appears as 'Riybg'. The name 'Congdon' also appears in these
entries as 'Congdon' and as 'Conydon'. The student will have to for-
give me if my guess, often in complete darkness, is not always exactly
right.   B.F.

No.1. p.83. Deed. 16 Jan 1640/1. Jno Congdon to Edward Persifull, for
3 bbl corn adds 13 acres to foregoing deed. This land near the dwelling
house of Persifull.
Wit: Signed   John Congdon
Thomas Sim'ons
    The mark of
Nich: N: Clark

No.1. p.84.
            A Court for Charles River County 29 June 1641 "att the
            Ordinary appointed"
Present   Capt Robt Fellgate   Capt Richard Townshend
            Capt Nicholas Martian   Capt John Cheesman
            Mr John Chew   Mr William Pryor

No.1. p.85
            A Court for Charles River County 22 July 1641
Present   Capt John West Esqr   Capt Richd Townshend
            mr Roger Wingatt   Capt John Cheeseman
            Capt Robt Fellgate   Mr Wm Pryor
            Mr John Chew

No.1. p.86
            A Court for Charles River County 24 August 1641
Present   Capt Wm Brocas Esqr Commander
            Capt Nicholas Martian   Capt Rich'd Townshend
            Mr John Chew   Mr Wm Pryor

No.1. p.86   Deed. 10 June 1641. John Bell of Queens Creek, planter,
sells Samuel Watkeyes his plantation and house in Queens Creek, formerly purchased from Wm Reynolds.
Wit: No signature shown.
George Clark his mark
   his mark
Wm W Robbertts

Note: Here again the imperfect handwriting. It is highly probable that
this name appearing as 'Watkeyes' may be 'Watkenes' - just plain old
Watkins in the modern sense.   B.F.

No.1. p.87
          A Court for Charles River County 20 September 1641.
Present   Capt John West Esqr   Mr John Chew
             Capt Wm Brocas Esqr   Capt John Cheesman
             Capt Nicholas Martian   Mr Wm Pryor

No.1. p.88
          A Court for Charles River County. 29th October 1641.
Present   Capt Wm Brocas Esqr   Capt Rich'd Townshend
             Mr John Chew   Mr Wm Pryor

No.1. p.89
          A Court for Charles River County 24 Nov 1641.
Present   Capt Wm Brocas Esqr Commander
             Capt Nicholas Martian   Capt Richd Townshend
             Mr John Chew   Mr Wm Pryor

No.1. p.90
          "At a monthly Court houlden for the County of Charles River
          the 5th of January 1641: "   (1641/2)
Present   Capt John West Esqr
             Capt Robt Fellgate
             Capt Nicholas Martian
             Mr John Chew
             Capt John Cheeseman
             Mr Wm: Pryor

No.1. p.91
"At a Quarter Court houlden att James Citty the Thirteenth
of December 1641"
Present   Sr Francis Wyatt Knt Governour etc
          Capt John West   Capt Thos Willoughby
          Mr George Minefie   Mr Ambrose Harmer

No.1. p.91.   Deed. 4 Jan 1641/2. Robert Bew of York in Virginia in
the County of Charles River, planter, sells Richard Carter of the same
County, planter, 1/2 of 150 acres in Charles River County "butting on
Rowlston first divydend North bounded with Hugh Allen his land on the
West syde and bounded on the East syde with John Peteets house Runing
Southwest into the woods a Myle". The price 600 lb tobo.
Wit: Signed   Robert Bew
Henry Jorden
 the mark of
Tho A Allen

Note: The name shown above appears to be correct as it is and not to
be John Peters. There having been a land grant to John Peteet.   B.F.

No.1. p.92.   Deed. 26 Jan 1638/9. John Utie of Utimaria in the County
of Charles River, Gent and Robt Booth of the same County sell Steephen
Gill, Chirurgeon, 100 acres, Adj S by "Mr Englishs Plantation" and adj
the land of James Bosouth, the land of Henry Willis,"soe to the fence
syde of the ould Forte feild", etc.
Wit: Signed   John Utie
Tho. Watts   Robert Booth
John Wright

No.1. p.93.   15 Dec 1640. Stephen Gill assigns the foregoing to Capt
William Leigh.   Signed   the mark S of
Wit: Stephen Gill
Phillip Thacker
John Hull

No.1. p.93.   3 Nov 1640. William Taylor confirms sale of foregoing
100 acres made by John Utie and Robt Booth to Stephen Gill.
Wit: Signed   William Taylor
Robt Taylor
Isaack Kinsmell

No.1. p.94.   26 Feb 1641/2. Capt William Leigh assigns above 100
acres to John Hull. The land described as "lying and being in Chees-
kaike".   Signed   William Leigh
Wit:
Richard Leigh
Tho: Dutton

No.1. p.95
> A Court "houlden att Charles River" 25 Feb 1641/2.

Present Capt Robert Fellgate   Mr William Pryor
      Capt Nicholas Martian   Mr Hugh Gwynn
      Capt Rich'd Townshend

No.1. p.96
> At a monthly Court for Charles River County 25 April 1642

Present Capt Xpoher Wormeley Esqr Mr John Chew
      Capt Wm Brocas Esqr   Capt Richd Townshend
      Capt Robt Fellgate   Mr Wm Pryor
      Capt Nicholas Martian   Capt Jno Cheeseman
                Mr Hugh Gwynn

No.1. p.97
> "At a Court houlden the 26th of Aprill 1642"

Present   Capt Christopher Wormeley Esqr
       Capt Robertt Fellgate   (sic)
       Mr John Chew
       Mr William Pryor

No.1. page 98 blank. The next page numbered 130.
     Records are missing from 26 April 1642 to November (?) 1645.

No.1. p.130
> "May the eighth 1652:
> Commissioners for the County Court of York are as
> followeth Viz't

Present Capt Nicholas Martian   Mr John Hansford
      Mr John Chew   Mr Edward Cheeseman
      Major Xtopher Chalthropp Mr Wm Gooch
      Capt Francis Morgan   Mr Thomas Harwood
      Capt Augustine Warner Mr Wm Hockaday
      Mr Henry Lee
      Capt Stephen Gill
      Capt Wm Barber

YORK COUNTY, VIRGINIA
Number 2

In the original pages up to No. 47 are missing. However there is a
transcript in the Virginia, made in 1894, which has entries from pages
45 and 46. Historians inform me that this transcript is not always to
be relied upon. Well, any interpretation of these early York records
is open to question. Certainly mine are. So we will include abstracts
of these few entries anyway.   B.F.

Entries of the year 1645. Probably for the month of November.

p.45. Transcript of 1894. Abstract.   Richd Bennett ordered to pay debt
of 450 lb tobo to - Belchambers.

p.45. Transcript of 1894. Abstract.   Richd Bennett ordered to pay Thos
Bennett amount due him.

p.45. Transcript of 1894. "Present Capt Chisman"

p.45. Transcript of 1894. Abstract.   Mr Wm Pryor sued by Joseph
Croshaw for false imprisonment. Jury awards Croshaw 300 lb tobacco.

p.45. Transcript of 1894. Abstract.   Order that - pay a debt of tobo
to Mr Wm Pryor at his dwelling house.

p.45. Transcript of 1894. Fragment. "Whereas Mr Henry Brooke stands x"

p.46. Transcript of 1894. Fragment. "that John Haward who hath x x ed
unto the said Rebecca Wallis shall make payment of x x lb tobo and
caske with forbearance and Court Charges x x x Jurnew within 5 dayes
next ells exec"

p.46. Transcript of 1894. Abstract.   - Brooke ordered to pay debt of
55 lb tobo to Richard Smith within 5 days.

p.46. Transcript of 1894. Abstract.   Thomas - ordered to pay debt of
300 lb tobo to John Hamor within 5 days.

p.46. Transcript of 1894. Abstract.   Tho Hart ordered to pay George
Baskpoole the assignee of Michael Saturwight a debt of 300 lb tobo.

Note: The abstracts from now on are taken from the original.   B.F.
The transcript referred to above is in the Virginia State Library,
Richmond, Va.

YORK COUNTY
Record Book No.2

AbsrActs from the original. Pages 1 - 46 missing.

No.2. p.47   Entry concerning John Thomas. He to answer suit of Mr Wm
Pryor. (1645)

No.2. p.47   Wm Light ordered to pay debt of 660 lb tobo to Jno Watson.
             (1645)

No.2. p.47   Order that Wm Todd pay debt of 325 lb tobo to Thomas
Nightingale assignee of Hercules Bridges.   (1645)

No.2. p.47.   Order that Wm Suite pay debt of 700 lb tobo to George
Beech.   (1645)

No.2. p.47   Order that Anthos Parkhurst pay debt of 300 lb tobo due
Amborsse Harmor.   (1645)

No.2. p.47   Thomas Borne arrested to answer suit of Thomas Ramsey and
not appearing "it is ordered utt sup".   (1645)
Note: "it is ordered as before"   B.F.

No.2. p.47   Order that Tho Hatfield pay debt of 460 lb tobo to George
Beech.   (1645)

No.2. p.47   Order that August Hodges pay debt of 280 lb tobo due Tho
Nightingale.   (1645)

No.2. p.47   Richard Milborne arrested to answer suit of Henry Corbell
and not appearing "it is ordered ut sup"   (1645)

No.2. p.47   Entry destroyed in the original. The transcript of 1894
shows "Whereas John Hartwell x x x -bert Beech and doth x x". (1645)

No.2. p.48   Entry mutilated. "x x Bennett was arrested to the Court
x x x and doth not appear it is ordered ut sup"   (1645)

No.2. p.48   Henry Brooke arrested at suit of George Beech and not appearing "ut sup".   (1645)

No.2. p.48   Elizabeth Hopkins the relict and admr of Geo Hopkins dec'd arrested and not appearing "ut sup".   (1645)

No.2. p.48   Order that Rice Maddoxe pay debt of 134 lb tobo due Wm Hawkins, this being the balance of a larger debt.   (1645)

No.2 p.48
        A Court "December the 20th 1645".
Present   Mr Wm Pryor
           Capt Ralph Wormley
           Mr Row: Burnham
           Mr Richard Lee   (or Kee)

No.2. p.48   Charles Smith arrested at suit of Thomas Ticknor and not appearing "ordered ut sup".

No.2. p.48   Order that Joseph Croshaw and Nicholas Clarke pay a debt of 600 lb tobo due to George Ludlowe esqr within 5 days.

No.2. p.48   Anthony Wady arrested at suit of Robert Lewis and not appearing "ordered ut sup"

No.2. p.48   Edward Grimes arrested at suit of Samuell Tucker and not appearing "ordered ut sup".

No.2 p.48   "Present Capt Nicho Martiau".

No.2. p.48   "Whereas Thomas Iles did this Court impleade John Leake for on hund: pounds of tob: and twoe barrells of Corne, due by bill dated the 14th of Apriell 1644 which was in consideration of Howse and grownd to plant on and Diett and washinge And for as much as it appeareth to the Court that since that bill past by the said Leake by reason of the late march the said Iles Leake and many others being drawne togeather and forced and made new Covenantes the said Iles Leake and the rest to plant in a generall way and to have all the Grounds in Com'on It - (The balance of this entry is destroyed in the original and is filled in from the transcript of 1894) - is therefore the opinion of the Court and soe ordered that the said Leake

1645

shall have in his sted for the said tobacco and corne and that the said
Iles pay the said Leake his charges within 5 days ells exec"

No.2. p.49   First entry destroyed. The 1894 transcript reads "Whereas
Edw Woodley was arrested to the Court to answer the suit x x not appeare
it is ordered ut sup"

No.2. p.49   In dif betw Thomas - and Capt Ralph Wormley deft., regarding corn which was fetched by Wormley from the other side of the river.
The Court orders "in respect the deft confessed that he fetched ever
the plantiffes Corne by order from the Leift of the County that the
said Difference be referred to the Counsell of warr".

No.2. p.49   Order that Wm Smoate (also as Smote in the entry) pay
debt of 1188 lb tobo due Mr Francis Morgan within 5 days. Morgan to
discount what he owes Smoate.

No.2. p.49   Order that Charles Smith pay debt of 580 lb tobo due Wm
Padyon within 5 days. This name may possibly be Wm Padgon.

No.2. p.49   "Whereas it appeareth to the Court by the generall
testimoneyes of Mr Rowl Burnham, William Gautlett and John Perrin
that the greatest part of the Cropp of tob: that was made by Mr'is
Dorothy Caynhoes servants and Robert Harrison Doth belong to the
said Harrison And that John Underwood whoe hath intemarryed the
said Caynhoe; as the said Robt Harrison alledgeth doth dayly dis-
pose of the said Cropp of tob: whereby it is likely the said Harrison
shalbe much Damnified The Court doth therefore order that the Sherr
shall forthwith Attach the said Cropp of tob: and that he see and
provide that the said tob: may not be Dysposed of till the next Court
or the said Harrison and Underwood agree uppon Division of the said
Cropp, or that the said Underwood put in sufficient security to the
said Harrison to be responsible for all Damages that may insue there
uppon".

No.2. p.49   Order that Thomas Deacon and Joseph Croshaw pay debt of
946 lb tob due George Beech within 5 days.

No.2. p.49   "John WoddBridge" arrested by Wm Gautlett and not appearing, ordered "ut sup".
Note: Although the 3rd letter in this name is a perfect 'u' in the
original, still it may be Wm Gantlett.   B.F.

1645

No.2. p.49   Entry mutilated. Mr Wm Pryor having formerly obtained an attachment agt the estate of Mr John Mottrom for debt of 8 lb of beaver, which appears due by oath of Richard Elrington and which was executed agst goods in the hands of Thomas Deacon, etc.

No.2. p.50   Entry mutilated. Gabrell Smith arrested at suit of - Bridges (prob Hercules Bridges) and not appearing "ordered ut sup".

No.2. p.50   In dif betw Capt Ralph Wormley and Martin Westerling for debt as due to the estate of Lewis Conquest. Referred to next Court and that George Gray who is found to be a party to the difference to appear, witnesses to be produced and the matter settled.

No.2. p.50   Order that Thos Wilkinson pay debt of 200 lb tobo due to Hugh Dowdy assignee of Wm Smote in 5 days.

No.2. p.50   John Sutton arrested at suit of Tho Lewin and not appearing "ordered ut sup".

No.2. p.50   Tho Deaco (evidently Thomas Deacon) ordered to pay debt of 234 lb tobo due Francis Wheeler in 5 days.

No.2. p.50   Dif betw Martin Westerling pltf and Capt Ralph Wormley deft, for a man servant, to next Court. Westerling to give notice to Mrs Mary Wormley who is joint executrix with Capt Wormley to appear.

No.2. p.50   Order that Charles Smith pay debt of 372 lb tobo due Wm Stookes in 5 days.

No.2. p.50   Charles Smith arrested to answer suit of Mr Rich: Lee and not appearing "is ordered ut sup".
Note: This certainly is "Mr Rich: Lee" in this entry. Not Kee.   B.F.

No.2. p.50   Order that Francis Wheeler pay debt of 1046 lb tobo at the house of Tho Chapman, within 5 days, to Joseph Hill, he being bound with said Chapman.

No.2. p.50   Entry mutilated. The following names appear on fragments. "by Tho Wilkinson Atturney of" and "that the said Hickman and Weaver"

1645

No.2. p.51   Mutilated. "Whereas x x was arrested to the Court to
answer x x of Sam: Abbott and doth not apper It is ordered ut sup"

No.2. p.51   Edward Grimes arrested at suit of Wm Hawkins "and noe
Accon as yett appeing against him", Hawkins ordered to pay Grimes 40
lb tobo for charges and the case ref to next Court.

No.2. p.51   Rich: Milborne arrested at suit of John Duncombe and not
appearing "ordered ut sup".

No.2. p.51   Tho Broughton arrested at suit of Nicholas Brooke and not
appearing "ordered ut sup".

No.2. p.51   A long entry. By a proclamation of the last Assembly
certain causes at the Quarter Court were referred to the County Courts.
Carbery Liggin having sued Charles Smith for 4500 lb tobo in the
Quarter Court, and there being no County Court, a question arises of
precedency, several judgements already having passed against Smith's
estate.
Note: The name shown in this abstract as Liggin, upon the assumption
that it may be the old Virginia name Ligon, may possibly be Kiggin.
One would have to trace this individual to be sure, which I cannot
attempt.   B.F.

No.2. p.51   Lewis Burwell, admr of the estate of Francis Carter dec'd,
ordered to pay a debt of 300 lb tobo for making the coffin and other
funeral charges, within 5 days, which is due to Francis Wheeler.

No.2. p.51   Thomas Heath to have an attachment against the estate of
John Clark for 806 lb tobo. "the said Heath hath had many writts
against the said Clarke and he cannot be arrested".

No.2. p.51   Order that Hercules Bridges pay debt of 1726 lb tobo due
to Sam: Abbott the assignee of Thomas Beale within 5 days.

No.2. p.51   Entry mutilated. Capt Ralph Wormley to have an attachment
against the estate of - for 1800 lb tobo and 10 bbl of corn for servants' wages.

1945

No.2. p.52   Mr Wm Pryor to have attachment agt est of John Holding
for 800 lb tobo and 5 bbl corn due Mr Rich Lee for wages of a servant
let to Holding by Mr Wm Litlewood decd, and assigned to Mr Pryor and
Mr Lee by Rich: Kempe Esqr admr of the said Litlewood.

No.2. p.52   Thos Bassett arrested at suit of George Ludlow Esqr, not
appearing "is ordered ut sup".

No.2. p.52   Wm Smote ordered to pay debt of 400 lb tobo due Jno Hutton
within 5 days.

No.2. p.52   Tho Hudson ordered to pay debt of 1500 lb tobo due from
him and Thos Todd to Thomas Wright, within 5 days.

No.2. p.52   Edward Shelu'rdine owing debt to Thomas Deacon, assignee
of John Earle, "by bill on hogg of twoe hundred and fifty pownds of
tobocc". Is ordered to pay Hogg or settle difference in next Court.
Note: This name Shelu'rdine. Or shall we say Sheluourdine. It appears
on pages 56 and 57 as Chelmadine. Now how on earth are you going to
pronounce it ? Or spell it in the modern manner ? My guess, just as
good as yours, for yours is going to be a guess in the dark too, is
'Sheldon'. Not Shelton, not Skelton, not Selden - but Sheldon.   B.F.

No.2. p.52.   Joseph Croshaw attorney of Wm Todd, ordered to pay debt
of 600 lb tobo due Thos Wilkinson within 5 days.

No.2. p.52   Dif betw John Broch pltf and Wm Light deft concerning
goods claimed by Broch from Light, referred to next Court.
Note: Once again there is a question of what name this actually may
be. Families named Broch and families named Brock may both be found
in the telephone book in Richmond in 1945. Both are of old Colonial
Virginia. The writing in this original is so imperfect that it may
be either - or it may be just another way of showing Brooke. All three
families lived through the three centuries in the same section. And
I might inadvetantly remark, with some slight contempt for each other.
I believe the Brooke family had some material advantage in the eyebrow
lifting contest - but they are all very old in Virginia.   B.F.

No.2. p.52   Richard Forde arrested at suit of Wm Suite and not appearing is "ordered ut sup".
Note: Once again the name Ford is exceedingly old in Virginia and
recalls that one of the family was murdered shortly after 1700 in what
is now King William County, then King and Queen Co, and in date of
these records, 1645, York Co. Disputes concerning the expenses in the
hanging of the murderer had to do with the recall of Governor Francis
Nicholson.

1645

No.2. p.52   Order that Wm Pitcher pay debt of 230 lb tobo due Thomas
Deacon within 5 days.

No.2. p.53   Order that James Harris pay debt of 8 bbl corn due Robert
Lendall within 5 days. The debt sworn to by Robt. Todd.

No.2. p.53   Order that Thos Sheppard pay debt of 200 lb tobo due
Joseph Hill within 5 days.

No.2. p.53   Order that Tho Heath pay debt of 500 lb tobo due Nicholas
Jurnew within 5 days.

No.2. p.53   Wm Burwell to have attachment agst whole estate of John
Davis Junior for debt of 2500 lb tobo. Burwell to put in security to
protect the Court for damages that may arise.

No.2. p.53   Nicholas Brooke arrested at suit of Richard Belchamber
and not appearing "is ord ut sup".

No.2. p.53   John Peade the attorney of Francis Browne confesses a debt
of 348 lb tobo to Florentine Payne. Order that Browne pay John Merryman attorney of Payne within 5 days.

No.2. p.53   Richd Bennett arrested to this and the last Court at the
suit of Robt Blackwell and not appearing, an order that he pay the debt
due of 330 lb tobo. also Court charges "and is in case of a Nihill
Dicitt ells exec".

No.2. p.53   Order that Henry Lee and Robt Bouth pay debt of 1150 lb
tobo due Richard Belchamber, ells exec.
Also another order. The same names. The entry mutilated. Also on p.54
an order regarding security for the two foregoing.

No.2. p.54   Order that John Wilson pay debt of 600 lb tobo and 4 bbl
corn due John Brooh in 5 days.

No.2. p.54   Order that Wm Gautet atty of Robert Haud pay debt of 300
lb tobo due Elias Wiggmore within 5 days.
Note: These names may possibly be Wm Gantlet and Robert Hand.   B.F.

1645

No.2. p.54   Order that Wm Smote pay debt of 854 lb tobo due Ashwell
Battin within 5 days.

No.2. p.54   Thomas Sheppard to have attachment agt estate of Thomas
Hayles to secure a debt of 200 lb tobo paid by Sheppard for Hayles to
Joseph Hill.

No.2. p.54   Order that Mathew Halyatt pay debt of 950 lb tobo due to
Francis Morgan.

Note: This name may be read 'Holyatt' and more than likely is actually
Halgatt. Now pronounce it as you please. For instance 'Holdgot' - we
all know people like that. Or perhaps 'Hellgate' or 'Hellcat' which
would perfectly describe some of my most beloved friends.   B.F.

No.2. p.54   Richard Milborne arrested at suit of Hercules Bridges and
not appearing "is ordered ut sup'er".

No.2. p.54   Entry mutilated. Half torn away. "x x was arrested to this
Court to answere the suite of x -w Wyate Admr to John Clark x x ut sup"
The transcript of 1894 shows this name as 'Edw Wyate', or as we would
have it Edward Wyatt.

No.2. p.54   Last entry. All names torn away.

No.2. p.55   "Whereas Thomas Waldoe was by the Churchwardens of the
new Poquoson presented for an abuser of the Church and minister, and
for not receiveing the sacrement The Court doth therefore order him
the said Waldoe to bring Certificate under the hand of Mr Charles
Grimes minister of the said parish of his reformation of the said
abuses to the next Court otherwise to be censured by the Court for
the same".

Note: The Colonial Church in Va. Goodwin. p.275.
This entry prepared by Dr. G. MacLaren Brydon.
Grymes, Charles. Admitted Sizar (age 19) at Pembroke College (Cam-
bridge), 1631. Son of - - of Ightham, Kent. Matriculated 1631. Minis-
ter at York Parish, York Co., as early as 1644. (Va. Hist. Mag. 1.346;
April 1920 p 133; Nov. 1920.)

No.2. p.55   Richd Wells arrested at suit of Edward Woodly and there
being no cause for action Woodly is nonsuited and to pay costs.

1645

No.2. p.55   John Coleman arrested at suit of John Leake assignee of
Gload Garraud and not appearing is ordered to pay Leake 20 lb tobo for
non appearance.

No.2. p.55   George Forde "father in law and Gardian to John Saker
sonn of John Saker dec" presents account for "the scoleing Cloathing
Diett and other nesessarys charges for the education and keeping of
the said John Sakers his estate". The account amounting to 2920 lb
tobo. Also presents an account of his ward's cattle. Court order that
Ford have all male cattle that falls from the stock in full satisfaction of the account.

No.2. p.55   Thomas Chapman having made sufficient proof in Court that
there is due to him 1200 acres of land for transportation of persons
hereunder named. The Court orders certificate be granted him for
Vizt

Tho Hinde	Wm Payne
Richard North	Henry Page
Wm James	Thomas Reynalds
James Hurleston	James Lewis
Isack Sanderson	Thomas Andrewes
Thomas Adkins	Eliza Smith
Robert Smith	Richard Doyddn
John Pratt	Ralph Boyer
Phillipp More	Thomas Roahds
Mary Greene	Rich King
John Wallis	Francis Hide
Wm Longe	John Bridges

No.2. p.56   Bill. Dated 10 Oct 1645. Wm Hockaday promises to pay to
Peter Simes 8000 lb tobo on or before 10 Dec next. Security being his
whole estate, servants, cattle, household goods, crop of tobacco and
corn, etc.
Wit: Robert Bouth   Signed   Will: Hockaday

No.2. p.56   P of A. 21 Dec 1645. Henery Brooke to Thos Heath to
collect debts in Colony of Virginia.
Wit: Signed   Henery Brooke
John x Sheirclife
Robert Deuty

1645

No.2. p.56   The following entry cancelled in the original and not
included in the 1894 transcript.
"A true and perfect Inventory of the Estate of Mr Francis Carter
Merchant deceased
Imprs - bill of John Davis for   00546 lb Tobo
Sr William Berckly his warrant the Receipt for   13542   "   "
       etc.   signed   Lewis Burwell Admr

No.2. p.56   Wm Todd authorizes Joseph Croshaw to confess judgt for a
bill of 600 lb tobo due Thos Wilkinson. Dated 18 Dec 1645.
Teste Thomas Beale.

No.2. p.56   "To the right Worp'll the Comit'rs of Yorke Countie
             The humble peticon of Christopher Stoakes Sheweth
that William Light and Richard Smith did become bound to your petition-
er Joyntly and severaly for the payment of eighteen hundred pounds of
tobacco and Caske", etc. The tobo to be pd 10 Nov last. The only paymt
having been 1 hhd of 300 lb paid by "the said Smith befor his death",
Desires judgmt agst Light and the estate of Richd Smith dec'd.

No.2. p.56   "Mr Bouth. Whereas John Griggs hath arrested me and you
at the sute of Richard Belchamber merchant my occasion urgent at
present that I cannot be at Court I desire you to present twoe notes
to the Court", etc. The entry is mutilated here. It continues " x x
Robert Lewis I would desir you to pay unto Edward Chelmadine seven
hundred and fifty pounds of tobacco and caske this my note shalbe
your discharge witnesse my hand"   Dated - Oct 1644
Wit: Signed   George GR Ruttland
Ar Willis

No.2. p.57   P of A. 29 Oct 1644. George Ruttland of "lin haven"
(Lynnhaven), planter, to welbeloved friend Edward Chelmadine to
receive 750 lb tobo from Robert Lewis of Queens Creek, planter.
Wit: Signed   George x Ruttland
Thomas Ramsey

The will of Robert Bew.
No.2. p.57

"Debts due from me Robert Bew being in full of what I am indebted
within this Colonie of Virg this 29th day of Octob: 1645
Imprimis   to Rich Pasmuch   090 Tobo
    "   to Capt John Chisman   320
    "   to Herk Bridges what he shall demand justly
    "   to Thomas Nightingall   120
    "   to Anthony Stanford for strong watters
    "   to William Pattison   020
I Robert Bew beinge sicke and weake in body but in perfect mind and
memorie doe make this my last will and testament in manner and Forme
Following
Imprimes I doe commit my soule into the hands of allmighty God my
Creator and my body to the dust from whence it Came.
Impremes I do Bequeth my temporall Estate wholy and soly to my
Brother Jeffry Bew making him sole executor thereof ". He to pay above
debts, etc. Dated 29 Oct 1645.
Wit: Signed   Robert Bew
George Wescombe
Charles Smith

No.2. p.57   Petition of Joseph Croshaw. That in July Court he was sued
by Mr Wm Prior for 6 bbl meal. That a settlement was proposed but not
accepted. Mr Nicholas Jurnew also being interested. That Mr Prior took
out an execution to the injury of his credit and he prays for a Jury
to settle the difference.

No.2. p.57   Entry mutilated. The transcript of 1894 shows "To Henry
Brooke mercht - A cravett agt the admr of the estate of Eliz Popley
widow. " 25 Jan 1645/6.

No.2. p.57   Entry mutilated. "Thomas Wilkinson to answeare a sute".
" x x of December 1645". Signed Thom T Hickman.

No.2. p.58   "John Meryman these are to desire you to get an order
of Court against Francis Browne for 300 lb of tob' and Caske and two
yeares forbearance which cometh to 348 and Caske or else - for the
payment of it the next yeare and likewise one hundred and twelve
pounds of tobacco of Mr Sewell ther as Mr Hopkins note of the pertick-
elers with his hand to it if past for it remembers it and likewise
fiftie pounds of Tobacco from the Estate of Mr Hanmore I paid him
- hhd of Salt lost to him at play and after on the same day at Kiquo-
tan I won fiftie pounds of tobaco of him I pray doe these things for

me at the Pawquoson and you shall command me the like not other but
rest
Aprill 21th 1645   Yours Florent' Payne   "

No.2. p.58   P of A. 19 Dec 1645. Francis Browne to John Pead, to
answer suit of John Meryman
Testes   Signed   Francis Browne
John Pead
Walter Gillerd

No.2. p.58   P of A. 9 Dec 1645. Wm Hodsson to Wm Browne to answer
suit betw Mr Prior and him.
No witnesses shown   Signed   Willa Hodsson

No.2. p.58   Deed. 20 Oct 1638. Thomas Curtice of the new Pocoson in
Virginia, planter, sells to Christopher Carlington of the same place,
planter, for 500 lb tobo in leaf, 100 acres at head of New Pocoson
River, adjoining the River on the north "and runing South into the
maine woods and by the gleabe land on the east side and on the west
side the said Thomas Curtis his land wheron he now liveth and in habits"
Wit: Signed   Thomas Curtice
Johanes Carter   his I   marke
Henery Jordaine

An agreement that Carlington shall pay the King's rent on the land to
Curtis.   Signed   Christopher Carlington
Wit: his marke   x
Roger Sadler

Note: This name is clearly Carlington throughout these entries. But
nevertheless I presume it should be Garlington just the same. B.F.

No.2. p.58. Entry mutilated. The transcript of 1894 shows it to be
an appraisal of the estate of Richd Winn, deceased, sworn in Court
in Dec. 1645 "Teste me Ro Bouth".

No.2. p.59   Inventory of the estate of Edward Percifull, deceased.
Dated 14 December 1644. (This date is possibly an error in the record
and may be 1645). Total value 3292 lb tobo.
                                Signed   Thomas Illes
"Jurat Coram me   John x Claikson
   John Chew   John Dauson
                                          John x Smith

Exhibited by Johanes Adyson

1645

No.2, p.59   Power of Atty. 17 Dec 1645. This is headed "Dme Ro Bouth".
It is from Joseph Hillis to Jno Perrin to represent him in Court.
Wit: Signed   Joseph Hillis
Will Grimes

No.2. p.59
Nathaniel Warren his bill of   100 in Rowle
James Harris his bill for   120 in Rowle
Mr Felgatte his bill for   620
Henery Lee his bill for   300 in Caske
Roger Sadler his bill for   180 in Rowle
William Light his bill for   600 in Caske
                                      - - -
                                      1920
Power of Atty. 11 March 1644/5. Henery Hedly to Arthur Price to
collect above accounts.
Wit: Signed   Henery Hedlee
Elias Wagmore
John Robison

Note: I'll be darned if Henery has'ent got as many little 'e's in his
name as I have in mine.   Beverley Fleet.

No.2. p.59
Mr Morgan his bill for   500 Caske
John Peted his bill for   400   "
Steven Gill his bill for   1200 "
Mr Gill his bill for   0350 "
Rice Madox his bill for   0790
                                      - - -
                                      3240
Power of Atty. 11 March 1644/5. John Robison to Arthur Price to
collect above accounts.
Wit: Signed   John Robison
George Rideell
John Ince
Henery Hedlee

No.2. p.59 Entry mutilated. The fragments show "Mr Robison received
of" Mr Hardege (?) 240, and "part of John Pettet his debt of 400 and
Caske"

Note: This fragment suggests that the name Pettit may have derived
from this confusion of tongues here in York County.   B.F.

1645

No.2. p.60
      Thomas Petman his bill for   50
      Steven Gasler his bill for fowrene shillings
      Mr Heath his bill for   330

Power of Atty. 11 March 1644/5. John Ince to Arthur Price to collect above accounts.
Wit: Signed   John Ince
Jaack Woose
(Prob a Dutch sailor. This first name may be 'Iaack' or 'Janck'.)

No.2. p.60   Receipt. 6 April 1646. Tho Jefferyes has received from Francis Wheeler the bills listed below to be collected.

Hercules Bridges	1000
John Evens	o720
Thomas Ramsey	0980
Wm Blackes	0300
Mr Felgatts	0250
Thomas Holdridges of	0200
Denis Steevens	0100
Mr Deacon and Robt Abrall	0380
Wm Coxe	0950
Wm Sawyer	0075
	- - - -
	4755

Wit: Signed   Tho Jefferyes
John Hull
Thomas Ramsey

No.2. p.60   Receipt. 6 April 1646. Received by Tho Ramsey, on a bill of Francis Wheeler, from Tho Jefferyes and Thos Best, 1600 lb tobo and cask, for which he will be accountable.
Wit: Signed   Tho Ramsey
John Hull
Thomas Jefferyes

No.2. p.61   The estate of John Saker sonne of John Saker deceased.
Imprs   to sooleing one yeare   200 lb tobo
To 3 yds of stuffe at 60 per yd and makeing
    the suite   190
To 2 ells of Canvis for drawers and makeing   070
To 2 pare of shooes   090
To 2 shierts   040

(continued)

The estate of John Saker, Junior, (continued)

To a Monmouth Capp	050 lb tobo
To a marking Iron to mark the Catle	050
To 3 yds of cotton and makeing his suite	100
To 1 pare of shooes	030
To sixe barrells of Corne for 2 yeares provision	660
To his scholeing one yeare more	150
To 3 yeares keeping his catle being 12 head the first yeare	1200
	- - - -
	2920

Actually adds up 2830 lb tobo.
Then follows a list of the cattle, 23 head.

No.2. p.62 (Note: The page in the original was eaten away by the
acid in the ink right at this date. However I can make nothing but
1641 of it. The 1894 transcript also has it as 1641.
        Deed. 11 January 1641/2. Capt Wm Brocas Esqr and Daniell Dick-
enson, both of the parish of York, sell to Capt Tho Harryson, for 4000
lb tobo in leaf, 200 acres in parish and County of York. It being part
of a greater tract formerly granted Capt Brocas "Butting and Bounding
northerly uppon the lands of Capt Nicholas Martiau and Capt Richard
Townshend, westerly uppon the mayne woods the measureing bounds to
begin easterly close adjoyning to a greate swamp and soe extending it
self between two swamps untill it meete with certeyne markd Trees at
the head of a run of water called the Midle Swamp being the uttermost
bounds of the said lands belonging to Capt Brocas on that part late in
the tenure of me the said Daniell Dickinson and my late brother John
Dichinson deceased", etc.
Wit: Signed   Wm Brocas
Henry Headly   Daniell Dickinson
Augustin Hodges

No.2. p.63   Deed of Gift. 19 Feb 1645/6. Edward Michell of the new
pawquoson in the County of Charles River, planter, gives to Robert
Sheild 2 cows.
Wit: Signed   Edward Micheill
Thomas Harrison
John Rose

No.2. p.63   Deed. 27 Feb 1645/6. Henry Brooke Jr, Gent., sells to
Nicholas Brooke Senior of London, merchant, 3 negroes (2 women and a
child) for 5500 lb tobo.
Wit: Signed   Henry Brooke
Michell Maisters
Nicholas Brooke Jr

No.2. p.64   Bill. 9 March 1645/6. Stephen Gill to pay Nicholas Brooke, mercht, 1150 lb tobo 10th Nov next.
Wit: Signed   Steephen x Gill
John Wyatt
Thomas Wilkinson

No.2. p.64   Bill. 9 March 1645/6. John Clyman to pay Nich: Brooke, mercht, 924 lb tobo 10th Nov next.
Wit: Signed   John Clyman
Tho: Harrison
John Griggs

No.2. p.64   Bill. 4 March 1645/6. Michell Master to pay Nicholas Brooke senior of London, mercht, 265 lb tobo on 10th Oct next.
Wit: Signed   Michell Master
Nicho Brooke Junior
Thomas Poynter

No.2. p.64   Bill. 30 March 1646. Nicholas Brooke Jr to pay Nicholas Brooke Senior 300 lb tobo 10th Dec next.
Wit: Signed   Nic Brooke Junior
Michell Master

No.2. p.64   Entry mutilated. Another bill of Nicho Brooke Jr to Nicho Brooke Sr for 4106 lb tobo.

No.2. p.65
          "Att a meeting by the Comitte of the forrest this 3d day
          of January 1645"   (1645/6)
Present
          Capt Samuell Mathew   Capt Thomas Barnett
          Capt Wm Brocas   Capt Christopher Calthropp
          George Ludlowe Esqr   Mr Rowland Burnham
          Capt Richard Townsend   Mr Arthur Price
                                     Mr Peeter Reddley

No.2. p.65   Order by the Committee that George Ludlowe Esqr pay 50 lb powder to York County on demand.

No.2. p.65   Order by the Committee that Capt Richard Townshend Esqr pay 10 lb powder and 30 lb shot for use of York Co on demand.

No.2. p.65 (3 January 1645/6). Phillipp Thacker sworn undersheriff
by Capt Richd Townshend at request of Capt Wm Taylor the High Sheriff
of this County.   Signed   Ro Bouth Clr

No.2. p.65
              A Court for York 20 Jan 1645/6.
Present   Capt Nicholas Martiau
              Capt John Chisman   Mr Robert Vaus
              Mr Wm Pryor   Mr Rowland Burnham
              Mr Francis Morgan

No.2. p.65   Order that Jeffery Power pay debt of 600 lb tobo due Mr
Zacray Cripps in 10 days.

No.   p.65   Order that Tho Nightingale pay debt of 288 lb tobo due to
Arthur Price the assignee of Capt Henry Fleete within 10 days.

No.2. p.65   Entry mutilated. This abstract is from the transcript of
1894. Thos Harwood exor of estate of Christopher Bartlett ordered to
pay a debt.

No.2. p.66   Order that Martin Westerlin pay debt of 600 lb tobo due
Arthur Price within 10 days.

No.2. p.66   Wm Harefinck ordered to pay debt 400 lb tobo due Arthur
Price within 10 days.

No.2. p.66   Michell Saturway ordered to pay debt 300 lb tobo due
Richard Evens within 10 days.

No.2. p.66   Jno Stevens ordered to pay debt of 300 lb tobe to Capt
Jno Chisman assignee of Henry Maggett within 10 days.
(Note: The uncomfortable thought occurs to me that this may be our
old and violent friend Henry Haggett. If so he is reduced to a horrid
little bit of vermin here.   B.F.)

No.2. p.66   Order that Mr Nicholas Brooke Jr pay debt of 1700 lb tobo
and 3 ells of Lockrum, in all equal to 2000 lb tobo, due Sebastian
Hill, within 10 days.

1645/6

No.2. p.66   Order that Nicholas Brooke Jr, who is security for Humphrey
Chaplin, pay debt of 537 lb tobo that said Chaplin owes to Tho. Gibson,
or produce Chaplin at the next Court,

No.2. p.66   Order that Tho Bassett pay debt of 911 lb tobo due Mr Wm
Pryor at said Pryor's house within 10 days.

No.2. p.66   Entry torn away. The 1894 transcript shows the name Edw
Dare in the entry.

No.2. p.67   Upon the oath of Edw Mikell it appears that Humphrey
Hamure deceased did owe the "sd Michill" 427 lb tobo, 3 lb soap, 2 pr
shoes and 7 pairs of Irish stockings.   The Court orders the supervisors
of the estate to pay.
(Note: A number of entries appear later, abt p.77 plus showing the
name of the deceased, and evidently generous gentleman, as Humphrey
Hanmore.   B.F.)

No.2. p.67   Order that Nicholas Brooke pay debt of 700 lb tobo due to
John Coleman within 10 days.

No.2. p.67   Order that Edward Woodly pay debt 200 lb tobo due Edward
Dare within 10 days.

No.2. p.67   Order that John Pownsey pay debt of 221 lb tobo due Richd
Belchamber.

No.2. p.67
          A Court 27 January 1645/6.
Present
          Mr John Chew   Mr Rowland Burnham
          Mr Robert Vaus   Mr Richard Lee

No.2. p.67   Upon oath of Nicholas Brooke senior, merchant, Amos
Johnson deceased owed him 18278 lb tobo. This appears from a letter
under the hand of said Johnson which is acknowledged by Nicholas
Brooke Junior, the administrator of Johnson's estate. Order that
payment be made with forbearance.

No.2. p.68. Order that Henry Brooke put in security in an appeal to
the General Court in a dif betw him and Arthur - (torn away)

1645/6

No.2. p.68   Order that Richard Duning pay balance of account amounting to 293 lb tobo due to Christopher Copeland within 10 days.

No.2. p.68   Order that Joseph Croshaw pay debt of 600 lb tobo due Thomas Basewell within 10 days.

No.2. p.68   Order that John Peteete pay debt of 360 lb tobo due Thos Nightingale within 10 days.
(Note: More and more as I work in these records do I believe that this impossible name is actually Pettit. This very day as I write, I note that a gent (in the modern sense, not gentleman) is hauled up in the Police Court in Richmond in violation of the liquor laws, who bears this ancient Virginia name. It somehow sounds quite right to me. Incidentally the Nightingales sing no more in Virginia.   B.F.)

No.2. p.68   Order that Walter Downes pay debt of 247 lb tobo due to Wm Barber.

No.2. p.68   Order that George Gill, attorney of John Bede pay debt of 1000 lb tobo due Henry Tyler within 10 days.

No.2. p.68   Now present   Capt Nicholas Martiau
                              Mr Wm Pryor

No.2. p.69   Entry mutilated. Regards an account of 1125 lb tobo due - Price. Apparently from - Lee and - Burwell. (Of course to Arthur Price from Richd Lee and Lewis Burwell.)

No.2. p. 69   In dif betw Steeven Hamlin pltf and - Brooke and Henry Brooke defts for 7 hhd tobo, it is referred to a jury who award 1 lb tobo to defts.

No.2. p.69   Order that George Westcombe, attorney of Hercules Bridges, pay debt of 1231 lb tobo due James Elcott within 10 days.

No.2. p.69   Jeffery Poore to have attachment against estate of George Higgins for 600 lb tobo "in regard the said Higgins cannot be arrested by the Sherriff".

1645/6

No.2. p.69   Order that Thos Bassett pay debt of 300 lb tobo due Geo
Ludlowe Esqr.

No.2. p.69   Thos Bushrode to have attachmt agst estate of Capt Thomas
Cornewallis to cover debt of 3030 lb tobo.

No.2. p.69   Order that Geo Wescombe attorney of Hercules Bridges pay
debt of 257 lb tobo due to Mr John Chew.

No.2. p.69   Last entry torn away.

No.2. p.70   Entry mutilated. Richd Belchamber to pay Geo – 345 lb tobo.
And further that John Griggs attorney of Belchamber shall make paymt
of the 345 lb tobo with 2 years forbearance.

No.2. p.70   Dif betw James Rogers pltf and Mr Wm Pryor deft for the
freedom of sd Rogers ref to a jury, which by verdict found for the
deft. Rogers to serve 5 months from this date.

No.2. p.70   Richd Duning formerly obtained an attachment agst the
estate of Francis Hardidge for 600 lb tobo, which was executed on the
estate in the hands of Nicholas Jurnew, etc.

No.2. p.70   Order that Geo Westcombe attorney of Hercules Bridges
pay debt of 1500 lb tobo and 6 bbl corn due Mr Richard Lee within 10
days.

No.2. p.70   Entry mutilated. The same names appear as in foregoing
entry. The amt of debt 267 lb tobo.

No.2. p.71   Nicholas Dale exor of estate of Ralph Watson ordered to
pay debt of 1000 lb tobo "for Phyicke administered x x in the tyme of
his sicknes" to Richard Dunning.

No.2. p.71   Order that Wm Smote pay, within 10 days, corn and cloth-
ing to George Codd who has served his time, he, Smote, being Codd's
last master.

1645/6

No.2. p.71   Order that Geo Wescombe attorney of Hercules Bridges pay
debt of 1250 lb tobo due in 1644 to Anthony West within 5 days.

No.2. p.71   Capt Nich: Martiau absent

No.2. p.71   Wm Hockaday having arrested Joseph Mosely to this Court
and hath no prosecution agst him is non suited.

No.2. p.71
           A Court 30th January 1645/6.
Present   Capt John Chisman   Mr Robert Vaus
           Mr Row Burnham   Mr Rich Lee

No.2. p.71   Order that Christopher Allen pay Thos Man assignee of
Michell Peasley a debt due of 350 lb tobo.

No.2. p.72   Entry mutilated. Henry Tyler who was security for Ralph
Eaten ordered to pay debt of 4 bbl corn to Steven Gill.

No.2. p.72   Richd Beetle was arrested to answer suit of Lewis Burwell
assignee of Luke Billington. He failing to appear, Thos Peach, his
security, ordered to produce him or pay the debt.

No.2. p.72   The estate of Ralph Watson decd being indebted to Joane
Floyne 300 lb tobo and 4 bbl corn, the Court orders that Nicholas Dale,
the executor, pay within 5 days.
Note: The name Teage Floyne appears in the early Lancaster Co records,
he being of Fleets Bay. It is possible that Joane Floyne nursed the
Rev. Mr. Watson in his last illness and wanted to go home - hence the
order for immediate payment from the estate, which was perfectly good
for it.   B.F.

No.2. p.72   John Sutton arrested for debt of 300 lb tobo and one
steer 3 yrs old, due Hercules Bridges assignee of Christopher Allen,
and not appearing, order that John Dawson senior security for Sutton,
produce him at the next Court or pay the debt.

No.2. p.72   Tho Sheppard arrested at suit of Michell Rooe who did not
prosecute him. Rooe therefore non suited.

1645/6

No.2. p.72   Henry Brooke ordered to pay 1000 lb tobo to Thomas Cater
for services done, within 5 days.

No.2. p.72   Mutilated. Fragments show "- Richardson shall have an
attachment" and "Geo Higgins as will be sufficient"

No.2. p.73   Order that Thos Broughton pay debt of 20 shillings (or
240 lb tobo) due Tho. Heath assignee of Nicholas Brooke Junior, within 5 days.
(Note: Which shows the price of tobacco at that date. B.F.)

No.2. p.73   "Mr Francis Morgan present"

No.2. p.73   Order that Anthony Parkhurst pay in 5 days debt "by bill
beareing date the 15th day of January 1643" for 6554 lb tobo, due to
Henry Brooke merchant. This being the remainder of a greater sum due
to be pd in 1644, Parkhurst having bound over his whole estate in
security.
Also Parkhurst is further indebted to Brooke 1300 lb tobo which Brooke
undertook to pay to Geo Hopkins late deceased, etc.

No.2. p.73   Order that Anthony Parkhurst pay debt of 320 lb tobo due
Thomas Bushrode in 5 days.

No.2. p.73   Order that Dictoris Chrismas pay debt of 300 lb tobo due
Tho Bushrod attorney of Henry Hawley and Mathew Bassett within 5 days.
Note: One cannot but wonder what on earth a person with such a name
as Dictoris Chrismas looked like ! - however a relief from the eternal
William, Thomas, Henry and Mary that our ancestors used for no other
purpose than to confuse modern genealogists.   B.F.

No.2. p.73   Present Geo Ludlowe Esqr
                     Capt Richard Townshend

No.2. p.73   The last entry destroyed.

No.2. p.74   "Whereas there was due to Thomas x x x x The Court doth
therefore order that x x x collect the said tob and corne from the
said fowerteene Mr Robert Vaus and his familye being seaven of them
and hath made satisfacon of on halfe of the said waiges to the said

1645/6

Tho Gibson of whom the Sherr is to receive the same backe again and
the remaynder from the rest of the said fowerteene which tob is to be
disposed of for the other publique uses and servis allready done by
men whoe have as yet not been appoynted payment for there said servis
Vizt to Robert Halsey in the first place his sallery due for his servis
done in 1644 att the Midle plantation Garrison"

No.2. p.74   Order that the Sheriff shall appraise sufficient from the
estate of Francis Browne to pay a debt of 348 lb tobo due John Merryman, and Browne to be clear from an execution for that amount according to Act of Assembly. Browne's estate consists of "a plantation for
three yeares on cow one Bedd coverlett and Boulster one pott and pestle".

No.2. p.74   Absent Mr Ludlowe and Capt Townshend.

No.2. p.74   Order that Francis Finch pay debt of 385 lb tobo due Tho
Bushrood attorney of Mathew Bassett and Henry Hawly within 5 days.

No.2. p.74   Francis Beetle arrested to answer suit of Tho Bushroode
who did not prosecute. Order that Bushroode be non suited and pay 100
lb tobo to Beetle.

No.2. p.74   Present Geo Ludlowe esqr
                     Capt Richard Townshend esqr

No.2. p.74   Difference betw Mr Ambrose Harmor, Admr of Tho Freeland
dec'd, and Eliz: Hopkins, Admrx of George Hopkins dec'd, for debt is
referred to the next Quarter Court.

No.2. p.74   In difference betw Abraham Turner plaintiff and Thomas
Chapman deft, concerning cattle and goods, Chapman appeals to the next
Assembly for trial and is ordered to put in security.

No.2. p.74   Last entry half torn away. The name Joseph Croshaw
appears and "refferred to the next County Court"

No.2. p.75   Order that Edw Woodly pay debt of 390 lb tobo due -
Hamor within 5 days.

1645/6

No.2. p.75   Francis Willis was arrested to answer suit of Wm Whitby who did not prosecute. Whitby non suited and ordered to pay Willis 100 lb tobo.

No.2. p.75   Joseph Preston admr of est of Wm Baulke deceased was arrested to answer suit of Wm Whitby who did not prosecute. Whitby non suited and ordered to pay Preston 50 lb tobo.

No.2. p.75   A Court 31st January 1645/6.
Present   Capt John Chisman
               Mr Francis Morgan
               Mr Robert Vaus
               Mr Richard Lee

No.2. p.75   "certificate to Robt Bouth 300 land". This written on the bias on the page and no further notation concerning it.

No.2. p.75   Order that Richd Wyate pay debt of 457 lb tobo due Tho. Bushroode the assignee of Robert Goodman and Attorney of Mathew Bassett and Henry Hawley within 5 days.

No.2. p.75   Whereas there was a suit commenced in this Court agst Nicholas Clark for 2559 lb tobo due to Robert Brasheire, by order of the Governor and Council in 1640 for trial. Clark then appealed to the next Quarter Court. He is ordered to put in security and "to pay Double Damages in case he be cast in the said suite according to Act".

No.2. p.75   Mr Wm Pryor ordered to appear and answer suit of Joseph Croshaw.

No.2. p.75   The last entry on this page destroyed.

No.2. p.76   Edward Adcocke to be pd 50 lb tobo for attending 3 days as a witness for Joseph Croshaw agst Mr Robt Vaus.

No.2. p.76   Jno Merryman attorney of Peter Walkington impleaded John Clarkson for renewal of a former judgmt agst Clarkson for 2575 lb tobo at a Quarter Court at James Citty the 15th of Aprill 1640. Clarkson claims payment and says he will bring proof to next Court.

1645/6

No.2. p.76   That Abraham Turner obtained an order of this Court in
Sept 1644 agst Thos Chapman for 240 lb tobo and 1 hhd which is not yet
paid. Chapman ordered to pay within 5 days.

No.2. p.76   "A caveat entered by the supervisors of Humphrey Hamnors
estate against the quietus of the administrators of Wm Baulkes estate"

No.2. p.76   A Court   "February the secound Day"   1645/6.
Present   Capt Nicholas Martiau
                        Mr John Chew
                        Capt John Chisman
                        Mr Richard Lee

No.2. p.76   "Whereas Thomas Deacon did formerly agree with the
Commissioners of this County to erect build and finish a prison for
the County after such manner and forme as in the said agreement uppon
record at large may appear and for as much as the said Deacon as yett
hath not performed the same according to his agreement this Court doth
therefore order that the said Deacon shall within one maunth next
finish the said prison at his owne cost and charges in respect he hath
received full satisfacon for the same according to the agreement and
for his default herein the Sherriff to take him into his custody and
to detayne him without bayle or mayne prise till the said Prison shalbe finished according to his former agreement".

Note: If there was such an agreement entered upon the records, then
this entry plainly shows that some of the early records of York Co.
were lost.   B.F.

No.2. p.76   Present Mr Robert Vaus. Mr Row: Burnham

No.2. p.76   Last half of this entry worn away. It has to do with
prison rules. "his said offence during the tyme of his imprisonment
lye in irons".

No.2. p.77   x x "that Humphrey Hanmor did by Will give to every on
of his supervisors and to there wives the sume of twenty five shillings
to buy each of them a Ringe". The Court orders payment from the estate.

No.2. p.77   x x "that Humphrey Hanmore did by his last will give unto
John Griggs howse and grownd for his life in the old feilds as also
twoe sowes". Order that the legacy be paid.

No.2. p.77   x x "by the will of Humphrey Hanmore dec that he gave unto
the wife of Arthur Seawell twenty five shillings for a ring". Order
that the legacy be paid Mrs. Seawell.

No.2. p.77   Mutilated. A long entry. That Mr Wm Pryor admr of the est
of John Scales and Edw Jorden sued Robt Bouth for 2300 lb tobo. Bouth
produced an account with Scales and Jorden showing payment. That by
oaths of The Wilkinson and Peter Richardson and also some part allowed
by Wm Hockaday attorney of said Pryor. Order that Bouth be cleared of
the account.

No.2. p.77   "Whereas there is due to Thomas Beale late Sherr of this
County since last yearo severall sumes of tobacco of Leveyes and fees
yett not rec". A Court order that Mr Beale cannot receive the levies
or fees but that they be collected by the present Sheriff or his deputy
and that he collect from them.

No.2. p.77   Mutilated. "The Court doth grant a commission of x x on
the estate of Ralph x x x security to the Court for the x x x"

No.2. p.78   Thos Deacon ordered to pay Richard Belchamber debt of -
hundred lb tobo within 10 days.

No.2. p.78   By will of Humphrey Hanmore he gave a sow to Jno Madison.
Order that the legacy be paid.

No.2. p.78   Order that Charles Smith pay debt of 2116 lb tobo, it
being unpaid balance of 2516 lb tobo due Thos Deacon, within 10 days.

No.2. p.78   Augustine Warrnor arrested by Ann Caudlier widow to James
City, and there referred to this Court. She not appearing to prosecute
is non suited.

No.2. p.78   Order that Charles Smith pay Tho Deacon, within 10 days,
a debt due of "three ells of canvis on pare of shooes of the tenns
and 340 size penny neales".

1645/6

No.2. p.78   Supervisors of the estate of Humphrey Hanmore deceased
arrested to Quarter Court to answer suit of David Foxe. The suit ref
to this Court. Foxe not appearing is non suited.

No.2. p.78   Mutilated. The dif betw Lewis Burwell admr of the estate
of Francis Carter deceased, plaintiff and Joseph Croshaw referred to
a Jury trial. The name of Robt Bouth appears in the entry.

No.2. p.79   Mutilated. This is greatly to be regretted for very likely
this is a bequest of early Church silver in Virginia. However all we
have is: "Whereas Humphrey Hanmore did by x x x x parish Church of
the New Pawquoson parish x x x x five pounds price". The balance of the
entry being an order that the supervisors of the estate pay the legacy.

Note: Now during the Colonial Period all wills of any estate in value
in excess of L 5. must be filed in duplicate in the Prerogative Court
of Canterbury. No, they were not destroyed. Having been kept for many
years at Somerset House, London, they were removed at the beginning of
this war and stored in the Welsh coal mines. Now many of our Colonial
Virginia wills, the original records destroyed here, simply must be
there.   B.F.

No.2. p.79   Mutilated. Half torn away. Seems to be that Mr Francis
Morgan, arrested to answer suit of Mr Robt Vaus for 700 lb tobo, is
ordered to pay.

No.2. p.79   Mutilated. Half torn away. Refers to and appears to be an
order that Nicholas Dale executor of - Watson, pay an a/c of 257 lb
tobo.

No.2. p.79   Mutilated. Refers to - Hopkins admrx of her late husband.

No.2. p.79   Mutilated. Half gone. Refers to Humphry Hanmore having in
his will left a silk carpot to Mrs Margaret Chisman, and according to
other like entries, the supervisors of the estate are ordered to pay.

No.2. p.80   Mutilated. The remaining words are meaningless. x x x x
"confessed the 26th of January 1645".

No.2. p.80   Mutilated. x x x "John Chisman and Mr Wm Pryor".

1645/6

No. 2. p.80   Mutilated. x x x "confessed a judgment to Henry Brooke
for three thousand x x x and caske to be paid with Court charges within 10 dayes".

No. 2. p.80   Mutilated. x x "confessed a judgmt to Arthur Price
attorney of John Ince".   This name Ince open to question. In the
original it is as though it were 'Inc'e' p ossibly even 'Juc'e'.

No. 2. p.80   Mutilated. x x x "confessed a judgement to Arthur Price
for sixteene" x x x.

No. 2. p.80   Mutilated. x x x "before Mr John Chew Mr Rowland Burnham
x x x George Wescombe confessed a judgement to Rice Row" x x x. This
name shown here as Row is shown in the 1894 transcript as 'Rice Love'.
It may well be that, or 'Rice Law'. It is really impossible for me to
decide definately. B.F.

No. 2. p.80   Mutilated. x x "confessed a judgment to <u>Thomas</u> Vaus for
three hundred" x x x.

No. 2. p.80   Mutilated. x x "confessed a judgmt to Thomas Deacon for
nine hundred x x tobacco".

No. 2. p.80   Mutilated. x x x "Confessed a judgment to Capt Ralph
Wormeley for " x x x.

No. 2. p.80   Mutilated. x x "Confessed a judgement to Nicholas Clarke
for nine x x tobacco" x x x.

No. 2. p.80   Mutilated. x x "confessed a judgment to John Robinson
for seaven x x pounds of tobacco" x x x.

No. 2. p.80   Mutilated. x x "a judgment to Nicholas Sebriell for five
hundred x x x of tobacco" x x x.

No. 2. p.80   Mutilated. x x "confessed a judgment to Thomas Harrwood
x x x Mathew Hawkins Junior for two thousand six x " x x x.

No. 2. p.80   Mutilated. x x "confessed a judgment to Rowland Burnham
x x pownds of tobacco".

1645/6

No.2. p.80   Mutilated. x x x "judgment to Thomas Deacon for" x x x.

No.2. p.81   Half torn away and difficult to read. The following items,
seperate entries, occur:
"George Leake confessed a judgment to Thomas" x x x.
"Rice Maddoxe confessed a judgment to" x x x.

No.2. p.81   Mutilated. January the 28th before Capt Nicholas M-.
"Bartram Oberd confessed a judgment to Capt H-". x x.
Note: For Bertram Obert or Hobart see Va. Colonial Abstracts. Vol.1.

No.2. p.81   Mutilated. "Christopher Copeland as security for Henry
x x a judgment to Thomas Curtis for three" x x x.

No.2. p.81   Mutilated. "Nicholas Clarke and John Coleman co- x x x
Rich: Belchamber for twelve hundred -" x x x.

No.2. p.81   Mutilated. "Charles Smith confessed a judgmt to Nicholas"
x x x.

No.2. p.81   Mutilated. "Eliz: Hopkins confessed judgment to Thomas -"

No.2. p.81   Mutilated. "Thomas Sheppard confessed a judgment to -"

No.2. p.81   Mutilated. "Geo Wescombe confessed judgment to Wm -"

No.2. p.81   Mutilated. "Edward Roberts confessed a judgment to -"

No.2. p.81   Mutilated.   "Stephen Gill confessed a judgment x x x of
tob and caske to Francis Wheeler" x x.

No.2. p.81   Mutilated. "Charles Smith confessed a judgmt" x x x.

No.2. p.81   Mutilated. "Rice Maddoxe confessed a judgment" x x x.

1645/6.

No.2. p.81   Mutilated.   "Robert Jmes confessed a j- x x Steephen Gill for 300 lb x x".
Note: Now here is a name open to any kind of an argument. The transcript of 1894 shows it as 'Inns', which it certainly is not. The best guess that I can make is that it is 'James' written in the cockney method of pronunciation. It is subject to correction in any interpretation.   B.F.

No.2. p.82   Mutilated.   x x "confessed a judgment to Hugh Rookes for 300 lb tobo: and -".   x x x.
Note: For Rookes see records of County Kent, England.   B.F.

No.2. p.82   Mutilated.   x x "confessed a judgment to Denis Steevens for" x x.

No.2. p.82   Mutilated.   x x "confessed a judgment for 308 lb tob: and caske to John -" x x x.

No.2. p.82   Mutilated.   x x "confessed a judgment to Charles Smith for three - " x x x.

No.2. p.82   Mutilated.   x x "confessed judgment to Richard Duning for five -" x x x.

No.2. p.82   Mutilated.   x x "confessed a judgment for 300 lb tob and caske to be x x x -as Ramsey within five dayes with Court Charges".

Note:
Rev. Ralph Watson.
The following mutilated entries have to do with the settlement of the estate of the Rev Ralph Watson. In Colonial Church in Virginia, p.314, Goodwin, but these notes prepared by Rev. G. MacLaren Brydon, this; "Of County Derby, cler. fil. Brasenose College, Oxford. Matriculated January 28 1619/20. Age 17. B.A., November 22 1621. Rector, Trusley, County Derby, 1629. Died in York County in 1645".

No.2. p.82   Mutilated.   x x "just inventory of the goods catles and chatles of Ralph x x x taken and apprased the 22th Day of January 1645" A list of 21 items follows. Then "Exhibit' in Cur Count Ebora secoundrd die feb: seq sic per sacrament Nich: Dale Ano 1645"

No.2. p.83   Mutilated. Half torn away. Is a continuation of inventory of the Rev. Ralph Watson submitted by Nicholas Dale. Refers to 30 great

books and about 50 books, "x x of them being lattin bookes". That is
about 50 Latin books. The name of Mr. Grimes appears concerning them.
Then follows a list of debts due the estate:
"Specialtyes Due to the estate"
Robt Todd by -   (Amounts torn away down the page)
John Thomas by bill
Mr Hugh Gwin by bill
John Clarkson by bill
Charles Smith by bill
Edward Grimes
Richard Smith
Abraham English
Capt Martiau
Ralph Horsely
John Holding
John Clarkson

A note written in margin "Some small quantity of Tob: and Corne due
for by those in the parish which the Church Wardens have not as yet
given any accot of"

The inventory includes "one blake serge suite
                        one old frize suite and one focke and a pair -
                        twoe yeards of blacke serge" etc.

No.2. p.84 Estate of Rev. Ralph Watson continued. Includes:
      "x x and 3 Lodgings in James Citty Nov: Court 1645   1o8
      and fees to Mr Bouth   080

No.2. p.85 Inventory taken last day of Oct 1645. A long list of items.
At bottom of page "Jurat' Coram John West".

No.2. p.86 Completely filled with list of debts due 1643 and 1644.
The names are most unfortunately torn away excepting:
- Corbell by bill   0011
- and Geo Gill by bill   0034
Edward Jordan by bill   0500

No.2. p.87 List of debts due the estate of Rev. Ralph Watson.
(continued)
Thomas Heath by bill   Amounts all torn away.
Capt Rich Poopely by bill
John Spencer
Edward Williams
Thomas Gibson
John Bell
Wm Crouch
Ashwell Batten
Wm Bates
                          (continued)

1645/6

List of debts due the estate of the Rev. Ralph Watson, decd (continued)

No.2. p 87
Thomas Henley   Amounts all torn away.
Wm Gantlett   (this name may be Gautlett)
Joseph Croshaw and for his boy
Nick: Sebriell
John Wayne
Robert Wilde
Leift Steelwill
Martin Westerling 4 persons
Capt Poopeley 15 persons
Thomas Saxe
John Thacher
Humphry Allen
Thomas Parnell
John Peynter
Richard Wells
George Leake
Geo: Wyate
Rebera Wallis
Fr: Peale
Thomas Watson
John Neler
John Calverley (Calverley)
John Perrin
Furnew for his wifes buriall in the C-   (this name prob Jurnew)
Jeerye Beery   (this name may be Jeorge Beerg)
John Utye
Robt: Bouth
Robert Lonyham (this name prob Longham although plainly written
                  Lonyham)
Richard Milborne
Richard Mayor   (this name is certainly Richd Major - which only
                   goes to show the difficulty in reading these York
                   records)
Jarvis Pilling   (possibly Pillivy and possibly later as Pollin, as
                   there was a John Pollin in York 1656. This name
                   also appears as Jarvis Pellum on page 195.)
Hugh Alden
Richard Wm.   (Subject to correction - possibly Win.)
John Hartwell

No.2. p.88 Has a wide strip torn away down the margin. Half of each
name is gone. The list continues the sums due the estate of Rev. Ralph
Watson.
- Hopkins   0049
- Henshaw   0053
- Croshaw by bill   0650
- Norer (?) by bill   0094

(continued)

Sums due the estate of Rev. Ralph Watson 9 continued)

-aley and Fr Jorden by bill	1200
-als estate do	0320
- Carters estate	0265
- Westerling - Caske at	0200
-ias Whiteheade	0375
-s Hardige	0080
-ry Brooke	0300
-y Brooke for Robt Wallis	0300
-y Brooke for Mr Parkhurst	1300
- Poopeley tythes 1644	0265
-ohn West by acc't	1528
	- - - -
	15488

No.2. p.88   Records in the settlement of the estate of the Rev. George
Hopkins, deceased. Of him we know practically nothing. Perhaps he came
over betw 1618 and 1623. There were two of the name. One at Oxford 1634
and one at Cambridge 1598-1600. The name appears to have continued in
Virginia.

These entries are mutilated - the page torn down lengthways.
Due to the estate of Geo Hopkins Dec' 1644 - 84 tytheable persons at
1 bushell per poll is 56 barr, 4 bush.

Rich: Hopkins	02		
Nich: Jurnew	03		
- Phillipps	02		
- Peale	00	1 bu	1/2
- Carter	03		
- Vaus	02	4	
- Westerling	01	1	
-rd Magor	00	3	
- -iutlett	03		
- Allen	01	1	1/2
- Burrowes	00	1	1/2
- Win	00	1	1/2
-hn Hartwell	00	1	1/2
-r Pitchfork	00	1	1/2
-	00	1	1/2
- -rnham	01	1	1/2
-d Beetle	00	1	1/2
-	00	3	1/2
-	00	1	1/2
-	00	3	
-	01		
-	03	3	

(continued)

1645/6

Items due the estate of Rev. George Hopkins, deceased. (continued)

No.2. p.89
from Peeter Bassill   00 -   (page torn away here)
from Thos Heath   01 -
from Thomas Henshaw   00 -
from Thomas Peach   00 -
from Elias Richardson   01 -
from Edws Wade   00 -
from Richard Harrison   00 -
from Christopher Abbott   00 -

Lost by 30 persons the yeare 1644 being souldiers at Midle plantation
and others run away out of the parish
(Note: This item is not exactly a 100% boast of heroes. B.F.)

No.2. p.89 Tobacco paid out of the estate of Geos Hopkins Cler dec'd
- - - Hopkins widdow and Administratrix of Geos Hopkins - - - 164-
Imp'rs   paid Capt John West Esqr for diett 3 yeares - one yeare for
mr Hopkins and on yeare for himselfe and wife - yeare for himselfe wife
and twoe servants
for one steere paid Capt West for his funerall -
for one heifer twoe yeares old Due to one of Capt Wests negroes and
paid Capt West for it   -
paid Martin Westerling -
paid Thomas Ramsey for a coffin and takeing upp the - in the Church
to make his grave there -
paid John Wayne -
more paid John Wayne -
paid Ralph Green for looking and bringing home - belonging to the dec
estate -
paid Wm Hodgson -
paid Joseph Croshaw for Thomas Deacon -
paid John Hammon for Wm Sawyer -
paid Joseph Croshaw for the use of Joseph -   -
paid for the Caske due to Sawyer and Moseley -
paid Henry Beech on hogd tob -
paid Mr Robt Wilde   -
paid more to Mr Wilde   -
paid to Thomas Peach -
- - (illegible) - -. Transcript of 1894 shows this as "pd Capt Wm
Taylor")

No.2. p.90 Page torn away down outside edge.
- -ansford on hoghd tob and caske (this name prob. Hansford) 0325
- Weaver   0810
- Lee for Phisicke   0206
-n Broch   1260
-en Gill for Diett Lodging Phissicke and Attendance in the
tyme of his sicknes   1000
                        (continued)

1645/6

Items due the estate of Rev. Geo: Hopkins, deceased. (continued)

No.2. p.90 Torn away down the outside edge.

- -ynhoe for supplying the Cure of the parish from - of the
dec'ts Dec till Chrismas   (Rev. Wm. Caynhooe)   0600
- funer sermon   0100
- Charges of letters of Adminstr   0065
- County Clerke 3 pounds percent on the Inventory   0460
-arges expended at Towne to gett Adminst   0100
- Wheeler   0110
                                                                  - - - -
                                                                  17159

- - acco't of Corne paid out of the estate of Geo Hopkins decd
                                                                  barrells
Mr Wm Caynhooe   10
Robt Wilde for his wages being Clerke of the parish   15
-ephen Gill   (Stephen Gill)   10
Francis Wheeler   10
John Foster Sexton
- Robert Bouth for findeing out what - and tob: rests
due from the parish 1643   10
Capt Rich: Townshend   01
- Wm Pryor   07
- John Chisman   06
-hn Chew   01
- - -
- - 45 by Eliz: Hopkins
x x x
Audited 1 Dec 1645 by James Corbett. (This name exceedingly difficult
to read. It may be Cockett or whatnot.)

No.2. p.91   Release. Part torn away. 19 August "the 21st yeare of the
raigne of our sov' x x Charles of England". Releases - of Virginia
from all debts, bills, etc. This person being "Tobias Dy- x x x and
haberdasher of London".
Wit: Signed   Tobias D-
The first name illegible. It may possibly be "Francis Moniuex"
Wm Brame
John Perrott

No.2. p.91 Most of this entry torn away. The part remaining all but
illegible. It has to do with the sale of 2 cows to Thomas Gib-, prob
from Capt Richard Popeley. In the original the witnesses names are
torn away but the 1894 transcript shows them as Thomas Smallcomb and
Thomas Heath.

No.2. p.92 Will of John Baxter. Dated "tenth of December at night".
Probated 6 January 1645/6.
All goods to Eliz: Clarke.
Lists debts due him as follows:
Thomas Beale 300 and odd
John Pellam 160
Charles Smith 90
Mr Lee a pair of shoes
Francis the Frenchman a pair of shoes.
Wit: Signed   John Baxter
John Peade   His marke
Francis Browne

No.2. p.92 Mutilated. Bond. 1st March - (year torn away). Christopher
Allen stands bound to Rich - for 700 lb tobo and 3 bbl corn. Allen
being bound with Charles Smith.
Wit: signed   Charles x Smith
- Wescombe
- Barthelmew

No.2. p.92 P of A. 26 May 1645 (the year open to question, the page
being mutilated here). - - to George Wescomb to answer suit agst him.

No.2. p.93 P of A. 7 April 1646. Richard Glover of Amsterdam, mercht,
to welbeloved freind - Lee of York in Virginia to collect debts.
Wit: signed   Richard Glover
James Besouth
Edw: Louicton (this name actually illegible)
Ralph x Greene

No.2. p.93 Bill. 28 March 1646. Sam: - to Richd Glover, mercht, 4400
lb tobo to be pd 10th Oct next. Witnessed by James Besouth.

No.2. p.93 Original entry practically destroyed. The transcript of
1894 shows it to have been a bill dated 4 April 1646 to Richd Glover,
2000 lb tobo. Signature missing. Wit by Richd Lee.

No.2. p.94 Bill. 15 Jan 1645/6. Francis Ceeley binds himself to pay
Richd Glover, mercht, 600 lb tobo on 1st Sept 1646.
Wit: Signed   the mke of
Augustine Warner   Francis FC Ceeley
John Duncombe
Ceeley likewise binds himself an additional 50 lb tobo. Wit: by John
Duncombe, Francis Willis, James Besouth.

No.2. p.94   Bill. 16 Jan 1645/6. Francis Ceely "of the parish of the
County of Yorke" binds himself to pay to Richd Glover, mercht, 2350 lb
tobo, on 10th Nov next. His whole estate bound in security.
Wit: signed   "Signum F C
Augustine Warner   Fr: Ceely the seale"
John Duncombe

No.2. p.94   Entry practically destroyed. Appears to be a bill of Robt
Holte of James City to Richd Glover. Detail, dates, etc. torn away.

No.2. p.95   A list of bills and debts due Richard Glover of Amsterdam,
merchant, left with Richard Lee in Virginia April 7th 1646.
(Note: The name written here is Richard Kee just as plain as day. It
no doubt is Richard Lee - but still it is written Kee.   B.F.)

Sr Wm Berkeley by bill with Caske   (Amounts all torn away)
George Ludlowe Esqr by bill with Caske
Mr Samuell Abbott by bill with Caske
Francis Ceeley by twoe bills with Caske
Capt Bridges Freeman by bill with Caske
Augustine Warner by bill with Caske
Mr Robert Holte
Capt Ralph Wormley
Steephen Gills bill resting thereon about
Francis Coole
Robert Kinsey
George Saughier
Mr John Chew
William Light
Mr Richard Lee   (or Kee ?)
Rowland Vauhan
Mr Nicholas Brooke Junior
Mr Wm Brooke Senior and Junior
Mr Henry Brooke by Arbitration and acc't
Mrs Mary Minifee by accoumpt
Wm Hinde per accompt with Caske
     For all fifty seaven thowsand ninty fower pownds of tobacco
     with Caske
                                    per me Richard Lee
Wittnes
James Besouth
Nick Satturthwaite

No.2. p.95   Deed. 23 of - - (month and year torn away in original
but transcript of 1894 shows Feb 1645/6) Richard Lee sells Edward
Yarrow son of Edward Yarrow decd, a brown cow and calf. Provision if
said Edw die before 21, etc. This mutilated entry seems to indicate
some some family relationship.

No.2. p.96   Bill of Sale. 4 Oct 1645. John Wayne of Hampton parish in
Yorke Co sells to Thomas Wilkinson a cow and calf.
Wit: signed   the marke of
Steephen Gill   John x Wayne
Wm Waters

No.2. p.96   Bill of Sale. Date torn away. John Wayne sells Francis
Flood a cow. Delivery made in presence of Steeven Gill and Tho -head.
                                            signed   John x Wayne
Names of wit: torn away

No.2. p.96-A   Bill. 23 Mar 1645/6. Capt Bridges Freeman promises to
pay Richd Glover, mercht., - lb tobo at a convenient place in James
City Co.
Wit: signed   Bridges Freeman
Robert Morslay
Wm Morgan
James Besouth

No.2. p.96-A   - Jan 1645/6. Augustine Warner promises to pay Richard
Glover 350 lb tobo at some convenient place "uppon the New Pawquoson"
on 10th Sept next.
Wit: signed   Augustine Warner
Abraham Turner
John Duncombe

No.2. p.96-A   Bill. 2 April 1646. Ralph Wormley of York promises to
pay Richd Glover 420 lb tobo at some convenient place upon the York
river, 10th Oct next.
No witnesses shown   signed   Ra: Wormley

No.2. p.96*A   Mutilated. 4th Jan 1645/6. Steeven Gill owes Richard
Glover - lb tobo.
Wit: signature torn away
Henry Brooke

No.2. p.96-B   Bill. 4 April 1646. Richard Lee promises to pay Richd
Glover 3000 lb tobo 10th Dec next.
Wit: signature missing
-ha Cavell

No.2. p.96-B   Bill. 31 March 1646. Nicholas Brooke Jr of Virginia,
merchant, promises to pay Richard Glover, merchant, 5292 lb tobo on
10th Oct next.
Wit: signed   Nicho: Brooke Junior
Edward Wyatt
James Besouth

No.2. p.96-B   Bill. 31 Jan 1645/6. Nicholas Brooke Senior and Nich:
Brooke Junior promise to pay Richard Glover 7500 lb tobo 10th Dec next.
Wit: signed   Nich: Brooke
Augustine Warner   Nico Brooke Junior
- Hockaday

No.2. p.96-B   Bill. 16 Mar 1645/6. Wm Light, Joyner, of York Co in Va.,
promises to pay Richd Glover 813 lb tobo.
Wit: names destroyed   signed   Wm Light

No.2. p.97   Bill. John Chew promises to pay Richd Glover 210 lb tobo.
Wit: signed   John Chew
James Besouth
John x Shertcliffe

No.2. p.97   Bill. 20 March 1645/6. Robert Kinsey promises to pay Richd
Glover 1030 lb tobo "made out of my cropp" 10th Nov next.
Wit: signed   Robert x Kinsey
Rich Lee
Samuell Abbott

No.2. p.97   Bill. 20 Jan 1645/6. Geo Saughier promises to pay Richd
Glover 344 lb tobo at some convenient place on the new Pawquoson on
10th Sept next.
Wit: signed   Geo Saughier
Augustine Warner
John Duncombe

No.2. p.97   Bill. 23 Jan 1645/6. Rowland Vauhan binds himself to
serve Richard Glover "the full and just tyme - - yeare beginning uppon
the first of November next ensueing".
Wit: signed   The mke of
Augustine Warner   Rowland -
John Duncombe
The above to be void upon payment of 300 lb tobo.

No.2. p.98   Bill. 23 January 1645/6. Francis Cole promises to pay to

Rich Glover, 400 lb tobo, on 1st Sept next. For security binds over
2 cows "being at Rye". The tobacco to be paid at some convenient place
upon the New Pawquoson.
Wit: Signed   Francis x Cole
Augustine Warner
John Duncombe

No.2. p.98.   Bill. 10 Dec 1645. Wm Wright, merchant, promises to pay
Richd Glover, 2700 lb tobo on demand.
Wit: signed   Wm Wright
Henry Brooke   "Vera Copia Rich Lee"

No.2. p.98   Mutilated. Appears to be a bill dated - - 1646. Sr Wm
Berkley knt, Governour of Virginia, promises to pay - lb tobo at some
convenient place in James City Co.
                                    signed   Wm Berkeley

No.2. p.99   John Hold- sells Edward Williams, planter, 2 cows. Dated
20th - 1645.
Wit: signed John x Hold-
Lewis Burwell
Wm Roberts
(Note: We presume this mutilated entry to have been the name of John
Holden. B.F.)

No.2. p.99   "This last of february 1645"   (1645/6)
The Inventory of Leift Smalecombe praysed as followeth
Imprs   20 armes length of Roanoke at   (all amounts torn away)
Im'   one parcel of old Cloathes one old
         small trunk without a key
         One Indian Gerle three yeares of age
         or thereabouts praysed at
                         Jurat' Coram Row: Burnham
                                 John Broch
                                 Thomas Browne

No.2. p.99   Mutilated.
"Cozen Henry Brooke
     These are to desire you on my behalfe to conf- - upon a bill of
mine to Mr Thomas - - - for three thousand pownds of tobacco - - - a
hundred more Kerborough Rigg- - him and I shall rest your very - - -
January the 28th 1645   Ni- - -

Note: It is most unfortunate that this particular entry should be so
mutilated that it is practically unreadable. That part of the name
shown as 'Rigg-' is more than likely 'Kiggan'. It would be interesting to know what the signature actually was.   B.F.

1645/6

No.2. p.100   A Court for York 25 Feb 1645/6
Present   Capt Nicholas Martiau   Mr Robert Vaus
                     Mr John Chew   Mr Richard Lee
                     Capt Ralph Wormly
(Note: The name Lee, that is if it is Lee, is written exactly like
Kee in this entry. B.F.)

No.2. p.100 Whereas John Griggs, atterney of Richd Belchamber, has an
execution agst the body of Hen: Lee for debt of 2200 lb tobo, and Lee
has petitioned the Court that he has not the tabacco in kind, and that
so much of his estate be appraised to satisfy the debt. Order that 4
men appraise his estate and "the said Henry Lee his body to be sett at
Liberty". Then follows a list of items appraised. Includes a "bote of
15 foote by the keele 3 oares".

No.2. p.100   Order that attachment be awarded agst the estate of Segt
Nic: Steelwill sufficient to pay a/c of 608 lb tobo and 1 bbl corn at
the suit of Henry Lee. Steelwill having departed the County without
License, Lee to be responsible if the a/c be not just and true.

No.2. p.101   A Court for York 24 March 1645/6.
Present   Capt Nicholas Martiau   Mr Francis Morgan
                     Capt Ralph Wormley   Mr Row Burnham

No.2. p.101   Whereas Francis Beetle was arrested to answer the suit
of the Supervisors of Humphrey Hanmore's estate for debt of 300 lb
tobo due by bill, and did not appear. Order that Edward Roberts, his
security, pay or produce the body of Beetle at the next Court.

No.2. p.101   Present Mr John Chew

No.2. p.101   Whereas Wm Keaton is bound by indentures to serve Wm
Hockaday the assignee of Henry Brooke, 5 years from 1641. The sd
Keaton absenting himself on the pretence of being free and also ran
away from his master. Order that he serve Hockaday till 28 February
next and for running away to receive 30 lashes on his bare back at
the whipping post.

No.2. p.101   Order that John Bell pay debt of 1080 lb tobo due to
Robt Bouth assignee of Walter Pitchforke.

No.2. p.101. Mutilated. Wm Suite was arrested to answer suit of John
Dawson and does not appear himself or by attorney. The name Elias
Wigmore appears in the entry, which is so far destroyed that it is
impossible to make sense of it. Wigmore is to be paid for something ?

No.2. p.101 Mutilated. Order that Elias - (Wigmore) - pay debt of 898
lb tobo to Wm Hinde.

No.2. p.102. Elias Wiggmore arrested to answer suit of John Dawson
assignee of Nicholas Brooke. Dawson not appearing is non suited.

No.2. p.102 Mr Hugh Gwin present.

No.2. p.102. Whereas a difference long depending in this Court between
Martin Westerling pltf and Capt Ralph Wormeley and Mrs Mary Wormeley
exors of the estate of Capt Christopher Wormeley dec'd, for a man servant due from the estate. The Wormeleys divers times summoned to this
Court, and this particular Court do not appear. Order therefore that
the Sheriff summon Capt Wm Brocas Esqr "whoe hath intermaryed with the
said Mrs Mary Wormeley" and Capt Ralph Wormeley to appear at the next
Court, they to have "tymly notice thereof".

Note: This long and involved entry irritates me. It must be included
to make the Abstracts complete. Now every Virginia genealogist knows
all the ramifications of the Wormeley family. All this type of entry
has to offer is slight additional evidence of the arrogance, complete
indifference to the written law, of the Council Group in Colonial
Virginia. The Wormeleys simply could not be bothered with such trivial
nonsense. B.F.

No.2. p.102 Whereas David Foxe obtained an attachment agst the est
of Arthur Makeworth for 6400 lb tobo on 25 April 1645. This was executed upon a pair of stillyards, 3 pewter dishes, 1 chamber pott, 1
broken ketle and 20 lb tobo in the hands of Thomas Harrwood, and also
2 young bulls in the hands of Arthur Seawell. But no replevy made to
Makeworth according to law. Order that Fox have - agst the goods
toward payment of the debt, etc.

Note: Let us hope that the wealthy and elegant Mr. Fox at least got
the chamber pott - such a necessary comfort for an elderly widower on
a cold winter's night. B.F.

No.2. p.103. Mutilated. By confession of Doctor Henry Waldron, he is
indebted to Arthur Seawell 2500 lb tobo. Order that he pay.

1645/6

No.2. p.103   Order that Mr Francis Morgan have an attachmt agst the
estate of Nicholas Steelwill for 700 lb tobo "in regeaurd the said
Steelwill hath privatly conveied himselfe to Maryland to live".

No.2. p.103   Order that Thomas Morley have attachment agst the est of
Leift Nich Steelwill for debt of 929 lb tobo "in regard he is gon for
Mary Land to live".

No.2. p.103.   Order that Thomas Adams have attachmt agst est of Leift
Steelwill for 1300 lb tobo.

No.2. p.103   A Court "March the 25th 1646". (1645/6)
Present   Capt Nicholas Martiau   Mr Hugh Gwin
               Mr John Chew   Mr Rowl: Burnham
               Capt John Chisman

No.2. p.103   Order that Elias Wigmore have attachmt agst est of Peter
Marks for security of a debt of - lb tobo, which he is bound to pay to
Wm Hinde.

No.2. p.103   Order that Edward Moleson be sworn Constable in place of
Edward Palmer. Mr John Chew to admr oath from which time Palmer to be
clear from service.

No.2. p.103   Order that David Fox and Richard Vau- appraise the est
of Ralph Pettymund. Jno Chisman to give them their oath.

No.2. p.103   Present Mr Fr: Morgan

No.2. p.103   Mutilated. Tho Harwood boing under execution at the suit
of Christopher Garlington for 360 lb tobo, his estate to be appraised.

No.2. p.103   Mutilated. Appears to be that Humphry Hanmore, owes, or
owed, Francis Willis 200 lb tobo for doing certain things at James
City. That Willis oweing him a larger amount is ordered to pay balance.

No.2. p.103   That Ralph Watson, clerk, deceased owed Capt Ralph
Wormeley 1371 lb tobo. Nicholas Dale, exor of Watson, ordered to pay
within 4 days, he having assets in his hands.

1645/6

No.2. p.104   In dif betw Augustine Warner pltf and Mistris Ann
Caudlier (or Candlier ?), widow, deft, which should come to trial
at this Court, is appealed by deft to next Quarter Court.

No.2. p.104   Francis Carter deceased owed Mr Wm Pryor 4229 lb tobo.
Lewis Burwell the admr ordered to pay.

No.2. p.104   Mutilated. By testimony of Phillip - and Richd Duning,
Edward Wright stood with Jno Holding deceased for paymt of - tobo to
Ralph Horsely, etc. Order for paymt.

No.2. p.105   "Christopher Abbott is this Day chosen Constable for the
Southside of Hampton parish and to be sworn by Mr Hugh Gwin".

No.2. p.105   Thomas Thrasher complains to the Court that Michell
Peasely his guardian "doth Dayly make wast and spoyle of tymber of the
Land of the said Thrasher". Peasely ordered to desist and appear at
next Court.

No.2. p.105   A Court 26th March 1646
Present   Capt Nicholas Martiau   Mr Francis Morgan
                     Mr Hugh Gwin   Mr Rowland Burnham
                     Capt Ralph Wormly

No.2. p.105   Capt Wm Brocas Esqr by note under his hand confesses
judgt to Sir Edmund Plowden knight for - lb tobo to be pd 10 Nov next.
Also 1000 lb tobo more for the service of a man servant from 8 July
1644 till 20 Dec following, as by bill of 8 June 1644. Also for a
servant sent to serve Nicholas Browne, etc.

No.2. p.106   Tho Adams confesses he stands obliged to Wm Howard as
security for Leift Nicholas Steelwill 1300 lb tobo. Adams ordered to
pay within 5 days to Henry Lee the attorney of Steeven Hamlin who was
assigned the bill.

No.2. p.106   In dif betw Thomas Shaw pltf and Capt Ralph Wormly deft
for 6 bbl corn "fetched over emediatly after the Masacre from the
house of Thomas Shaw on the north side of Yorke river". This confessed
by Wormeley who states it was brought by order of the Lieutenant. Capt
Wormeley ordered to pay plus 50 lb tobo expense.

1646

No.2. p.106   Augustine Hodges stands indebted to Wm Padeson, assignee
of John Pellam, for 700 lb tobo. Order that he pay.

No.2. p.106   By note under the hand of Nicholas Brooke Jr, he promised
to pay Eliz: Hopkins widow, admr of Geo Hopkins deceased, for the burial
of Mr Edw Brooke deceased. "whoo was buryed in the Chancell". Brooke Jr
is ordered to pay Mrs Hopkins 300 lb tobo.

No.2. p.106   Henry Lee obtained an attachmt agst the est of Lt. Nicho:
Steelwill in Feb Court which was executed on 1100 lb tobo in hands of
Francis Willis, etc.

No.2. p.107   In dif betw Francis Willis admr of Tho Simons decd pltf
and Tho Kerby deft, concerning cattle, Kerby appeals to next Quarter
Court and is ordered to put in security.

No.2. p.107   Mutilated. Wm Hodgson is indebted to Mr Wm Pryor, by
specialty as security for Elizebeath - for 8 bbl corn to be paid in
Hampton - (prob. parish) -. Order for payment.

No.2. p.107   George Brocas to have comm of admr on estate of William
Quoke, he being a creditor.

No.2. p.107   Capt Jno West Esqr to have comm of admr on estate of Tho:
Doe deceased for use of Ann Doe his daughter, according to the will of
said Doe proved in Court.

No.2. p.107   By specialty under the hand of Thos Hickman and of James
Harris they are indebted to Robt Kinsey 1500 lb tobo. Hickman ordered
to pay within 5 days.

No.2. p.107   Mutilated. The name Samuel Tucker appears as having
arrested - on an account.

No.2. p.108   Christopher Allen arrested at suit of Anthony Stanfforde
and sd Stanford not appearing is non suited.

No.2. p.108   Mr Nicho: Brooke Jr appealing upon petition of Thomas
Stegg Esqr to next Quarter Court is ordered to put in security.

1646

No.2. p.108   Hercules Bridges arrested to answer suit of Nich: Jurnew.
Jurnew not appearing is non suited.

No.2. p.108   A Court 27 March 1646   (1646)
Present   Capt John West Esqr   Mr Row: Burnham
                   Capt Nicholas Martiau   Mr Rob't Vaus
                   Mr Hugh Gwin

No.2. p.108   In dif betw Joseph Croshaw pltf and Mr Robt Vaus deft,
Vaus appeals to next Quarter Court and ordered to put in security.

No.2. p.108   John Adison "he being a soulder at forte Royall",
petitions to be clear from the Country levy. This granted.

No.2. p.108   Wm Hockaday arrested at suit of Tho Saxe. Saxe not
appearing is non suited.

No.2. p.109   Jeffery Power obtained an attachmt agst the est of Geo
Higgins for 600 lb tobo. This executed upon a cow, heifer and a calf.

No.2. p.109   Charles Smith, John Clarkson and Robt Todd impleaded by
Nicholas Dale exor of Ralph Watson dec'd for debts due are ordered to
come to a settlement.

No.2. p.109   Comm of admr granted Robt Vaus on estate of Geo Peterson
deceased as a creditor.

No.2. p.109   Such cattle of Jeffery Power to be appraised as will
satisfy a debt of 600 lb tobo due Mr Cripps.

No.2. p.109   Mutilated. Order that Robt Vaus have attachmt agst est
of Francis Hardidge for debt of 1025 lb tobo.

No.2. p.109   Entry half gone. Has to do with a debt due from Francis
Hardidge to Richard —

No.2. p.110   Capt Derrick Derrickson to have attachmt agst the est
of Lt Nicho: Steelwill for 2132 lb tobo.

No.2. p.110   In difference at last Court betw John and George Jonson
pltfs and Christopher Copeland deft for 50 acres of land which Copeland
"Did long since sell to the plaintiffs and past bill of sale for the
same therein binding himself to make good the said Land", deliver the
patent, etc. Copeland not appearing is ordered to make good the land
or return 1400 lb tobo with interest.

No.2. p.110 Unfinished cases at this Court to be put off until 1st of
May "Easter is so ny at hand".

No.2. p.110   Wm Todd by his attorney Joseph Croshaw confesses judgmt
to Saml Snead for 300 lb tobo.

No.2. p.110   Wm Hookaday atty of Obedd Wms confesses judgmt to Wm
Todd for 300 lb tobo.

No.2. p.110   P of A. - March 1646. Obed Wms to "my frend" Wm Hookaday
to conf judgt in a debt due Wm Todd
Wit: names torn away.   signed   Obed Wms

No.2. p.111   Judgmts confessed 24th March 1645/6 before Capt Nicholas
Martiau and Mr John Chew.
David Doehart 266 lb tobo due to Thomas Deacon
John Hutton 1300 lb tobo due Robt Kinsey
David Doehart 500 lb tobo due Jno Holding
Jno Bide 1403 lb tobo due Mr Wm Pryor
Tho Hatfield due Mr Wm Pryor 607 lb tobo.
Henry Brooke due 4000 lb tobo to Mr Wm Pryor
Wm Blackey due 661 lb tobo to Mr Wm Pryor

No.2. p.111 Judgmts confessed 23 March 1646 (actually 1645/6) before
Capt Nich Martiau and Mr Jno Chew.
Thomas Bremer 300 lb tobo to Capt Henry Fleet
Francis Willis admr to Tho Simons dec'd, 500 lb tobo to Sir Edmund
     Plowden
Robert Todd, 300 lb tobo to - (torn away) -.

No.2. p.112   Judgments confessed "before Mr Hugh Gwin and Mr Row:
Burnham".
Thos Sheppard and Thos Hayles 494 lb tobo to Mr Wm Pryor
Thos Taylor 250 lb tobo to Thos Deacon
Thos Taylor 1200 lb tobo to Mr Wm Pryor

                              (continued)

1646

Judgmts confessed beore Mr Hugh Gwin and Mr Row: Burnham (continued)
No.2. p.112
Thos Kerby by his attorney Mr Wm Whitby to Mr Richd Lee 250 lb tobo
Edwd Woodly 400 lb tobo to Mr Richd Lee
Thomas Beale 2000 lb tobo to be paid in "porke or catle" due by bill
        dated 3 Feb 1645/6 to Arthur Price. Also 180 lb tobo as foregoing
John Holding 230 lb tobo to Nicholas Dale exor of Ralph Watson,Clerk.

No.2. p.112   P of A. 23 March 1645/6. David Doeharte to Phillipp
Wooden to ack judgt in 2 suits, one of Jno Holding and the other of
Thos Deacon.
Wit: names mutilated,   signed   the mark of
appears to be - Abeall   x
                                            David Doeharte

No.2. p.113   P of A. 16 Feb 1645/6. "Mary Minifie widdow and execu-
trix of George Menefie late of Buckland Esqr dec'd" to "my trusty and
Loveing Freind Rowland Burnham" to collect a/cs due in York Co.
Wit: signed   Mary Menefie
John Bishoppe
Humphry Lister

No.2. p.113   Certificate dated 13 Feb 1645/6. From the Court of
Charles City County that George Menefie of Buckland esqr deceased,
did, by his will, appoint his wife Mistress Mary Menefie his executrix.
That the will was probated at a Court held 20 Jan 1645/6.
                                signed   Tho: Stegge
                                          John Bishoppe
Test Hoell Price   Thomas Drewe

(Note: This is one of the most interesting items in these records.B.F.)

No.2. p.114   P of A. 17 March 1645/6. Wm Blackey writes to Mr Bouth
appointing his friend Wm Hockaday his attorney to ack a debt of 61 lb
tobo to Mr Pryor.
Wit: signed   William Blackey
Tho.   TH Holmes

No.2. p.114   P of A. 16 March 1645/6. Thomas Hatfield writes to Mr
Bouth appointing his friend Wm Hockaday his attorney to ack a debt of
670 lb tobo to Mr Pryor, for which his crop and a black cow are bound.
Wit: signed   Tho Hatfield
Edward Jenkins   his T marke

1646

No.2. p.114   P of A. 17 March 1645/6. John Bide writes Mr Bouth
appointing his friend Wm Hookaday his attorney to ask a debt of 1403
lb tobo to Mr Pryor for which his plantation, houseing, crop and 3
cows are bound.
With: signed   John IB Bide
Michell Victor   his mark

No.2. p.114   A letter from Henry Brooke dated 23 March 1645/6 to "Mr
Le" explaining that he would not have failed to come to Court, but as
Mr Hookaday knew, he was kept away by other business. Has to do with
acknowledging a debt of 4000 lb tobo which he apparently in some way
owes "Mistress Popeley to Mr Pryor". This mutilated entry is difficult
to abstract. A transcript would mean nothing. The name Savage appears.

No.2. p.115   An entry regarding a suit brought by Sir Edmund Plowden
against someone, name not shown, who does not appear. "Ordered by the
Court to be subscribed by Ro Bouth Clr Cur".

No.2. p.115   "I Desire that an order may be entered for the payment
of the tobacco due to Sr Edmund Plowden by the last of November next
with forbearance"   signed   W.Brocas
26 March 1646.

No.2. p.115   "Nicholas Browne of the Cacke river aged forty yeares or
there abouts maketh oath that Sr Edmund Plowden knight complayneing
that Capt Wm Brocas had fayled to send him a servant to waite on him
and that under twoe hundred pownds of tobacco a mounth he could not
hire any fitted and cloathed
      This Depo't for a thowsand pownds of tobacco and caske about the
Eight day of July last past sold to the said Sr Edmund Plowden Thomas
Waggett his tyme to serve him - for five Mounthes and more
Jurat' in Cur   Nic Browne
Teste me
Tho. Cely

Note: Burke. "PLOWDEN (Plowden, co. Salop; derived from Roger Plowden,
of Plowden, a crusader at the seige of Acre in 1194, who is stated to
have received for his services there, the augmentation to his arms of
the fleurs-de-lis. Of this ancient family was the learned Serjeant
Edmund Plowden, of Plowden, so eminent as a lawyer temp. Queens Mary
and Elizabeth) Az. a fesse dancettee, the two upper points terminat-
ing in fleurs-de-lis or. Crest. On a mount vert a buck pass.sable,
attired or."

No.2. p.115   Humphry Sayle sells Humphry Walden 25 acres of land
"which was for my personall adventure untc Cheeskiacke". Dated 4th
Dec 1635. "This Land Lieth on the est side of Wests Creeke nere the
Head thereof"
Wit: Signature torn away
Oliver Downes
Anthony Watts

No.2. p.115   Mutilated - half gone. Deed. 14 Feb 1642/3. Capt John
West sells a parcel of land to Anthony Wayde. This land "bounded from
the mayne -" x x x "first Inlett that -". Then the name appears in
the body of the deed plainly as "Anthony Wady".
Wit: Signed   John West
Henry Lee
Wm W Sawyer
                          March 26th 1646
"This was accknowledged in the presence of the Court to be the Reall
Act and deed and Just sale of Capt John West Esqr And that the said
Capt John West Did receive a valuable consideration for the same of
and from Anthony Wadye
          Teste me Ro Bouth Clr Cur "

No.2. p.116   Anthony Wadye assigns interest in above land to Robert
Holte. 6th Jan 1643/4.   Signed   Snthony Wady
Wit: A
John Eaton   his mke
Richard x James
     his mark

No.2. p.116   Robert Holt assigns his right in above land to Derreck
Derreckson. 20 March 1646/   (1645/6) No signature or witnesses shown.
"Teste me Ro Bouth Clr Cur"

No.2. p.117   14th April 1646. Thomas Beale of York Parish, in consideration of 1200 lb tobo due from him to Capt Wm Taylor "high Sherriffe
of Yorke County the last yeare 1645", for Country Levies, which tobo
being assigned over to George Ludlowe Esqr, and by the said Capt Taylor
according to Act of Assembly. Beale now mortgages his cattle as securit;
for paymt on 10th Dec next.
Wit: Signed   Tho Beale
Wm Whitby
Thomas Wallis

No.2. p.117   Receipt. 20 March 1642/3. - Brassure to John Clarkson
of York in Virginia, 1329 lb tobo in full satisfaction of all debts.
And "appoynte Capt Wm Leigh my Lawfull Atturney" to deliver Clarkson's
specialty to "Owen Loyde my now Atturney whoe is to deliver it freely
upp to the said Clarkson"   Signed   "Brassure"
Wit: Arthur Price

No.2. p.117   Mutilated. P of A. Dated at Capt John West's house - -
1644. Thomas Doe to Capt John West to administer his estate "for the
good of my Daughter Ann Doe". Also an order for writings in a chest in
the house of Steeven Giles in James Towne to be delivered to Capt West.
"now finding the tymes Dangerous giveing my x x x to goe over the
forrest alone"
Wit: Signature torn away
Willi Hodgson
"Probat' in Cur.Court Eboris vicesimo x x"

No.2. p.118   Bill. 17 March 1645/6. Richard Bennett of <u>Yorke</u> in the
<u>County of Charles River</u>, planter, stands indebted to Thos Harwood of
same County, 900 lb tobo to be pd last of Nov next at the "now Dwell-
ing howse of the sd Bennett". Whole crop of tobo as security.
Wit: signed   Richard Bennett his mke
Arthur Seawell
Edward Michell

Note: Thus the confusion of names. I do not presume this to be the
Puritan who later became Governor of Virginia. I don't think it could
have been.   B.F.

No.2. p.118   Wm Smote of Hampton, "bootewright", (this certainly must
mean 'boatwright') binds his whole estate to Joseph Hill to secure a
debt of 860 lb tobo that the said Joseph stands bound with him to
Ashell Batten. Dated 8 March 1645/6.
Wit: signed   the marke of
the mke of   Wm W Smote
Ashwell x Batten
the mke of
John x Bide

No.2. p.118   P of A. 12 Dec 1645. David Jones of Willoy to Steephen
Hamlin to "recover a debt of Nicholas - Thomas Adams and Robert
Bouth", etc. Entry mutilated. Not clear.
Wit: signed   David Jones
names destroyed

No.2. p.119   P of A. 5 March 1645/6. Steeven Hamlin to Henry Lee to
collect debts in York River.
Wit: signed   Steeven Hamlin
Thos x Morland
John Conell

No.2. p.119   Will of Richard Smith of the parish of York in Virginia.
Dated 24 March 1644/5. Whole estate to wife. Her name appears in the

1646

The will of Richard Smith (continued)

codicil. see below.
Wit: Signed   Rich Smith
Henry Pucoke
James x Winddral (possibly 'Wiuddral ?)

Codicil. Dated 18 Nov 1645. That wife Alce is now with child. If the
child lives it to have half the estate.
Wit: Signature torn away
John x Holding
Lawr: Hulett

No.2. p.120   Deed. 8 Nov 1643. Joseph Croshaw of Queens Creek, planter,
sells Edward Adcocke of Martins hundred, planter, 250 acres in Queens
Creek, part of a dividend of 350 acres. Adjs land of Wm Ireland, etc.
Wit: Signed   Joseph Croshaw
Wm Burwell
Peeter Rainson

No.2. p.120   "I John Hartwell doe by theise presents acknowledge that
I am hartyly sorry for the scandall and aspersion by me layed upon Wm
Todd and his wife and Edward Adcocke and his wife and I doe hereby
acknowledge my fault, as wittnes my hand this last day of July 1646"
Wit: Signed   the marke of
John Underwood   H
Lewis Burwell   John Hartwell
Joseph Croshaw
Wm Gantlett (or Gautlett ?)

No.2. p.120   Elizabeth Popeley gives a heifer to Bennett Gill, her
heirs, etc, 1 April 1645.
                              Signed   Eliz: Popeley

No.2. p.121   A Court at Yorke 10 April 1646
              "By the Leifts and Deputy Leiftents"
Present   Capt John West   Mr John Chew
                  Capt Wm Brocas   Capt John Chisman
                  Geo Ludlowe   Capt Wm Taylor
                  Capt Rich Townshend

No.2. p.121   An order from James Citty dated 2 March 1645/6, that the
Lieutenants and Deputy Lieutenants press 16 men to march against the

Indians under the command of Leift Francis Poyethres ant to be ready
at place of Randevous the 20th of this April to attend this service,
Provision to be made for protection of their crops. They to be pd 100
lb tobo for every day wasted, etc.

No.2. p.121   P of A. Derrick Derickson of Grast in Holland to Edward
Peeters of York in Virginia to collect debts. Dated 15th -- -- month and
year torn away.
Wit: Signed   Derrick Derickson
Steph G Gill
Thomas Hatton

No.2. p.122   A Court 13 April 1646
Present   Capt John West
                   Capt Wm Brocas
                   Geo Ludlowe
                   Capt Richard Townshend

No.2. p.122   By an order of the last Grand Assembly dated 20th March
1645/6, with consent of Edw Wyate Admr of the estate of John Clarke
deceased, plaintiff, and Capt Robt Higginson, deft, that the said
Wyate is to enjoy 50 pole breadth of land adjoining the land of Honry
Tylor, "sittuate on the midle plantacon pales for ever and the said
Higginson to injoye the howse he nowe lives in with an moyety of a
tobacco howse till the tenth day of December next and what howses the
said Capt Higginson shall build or repaire upon the said land this
present yeare at the surrender thereof to the said Wyate at the time
aforesaid", Wyate to pay him in tobo or work as valued by Wm Davis and
Henry Tylor, Wyate and Higginson to plant upon the land this year
according to the proportion of their hands. The entry also refers to
50 pole of land next adjoining thereto belonging to Mr Nich: Brookes.
A long entry, etc, etc.
A second entry follows in which above is referred to the Commissioners
of York County.
                                        Signed by
                                             "John Corker Clk to
                                              The Burgesses"

No.2. p.123   A Court for York 25 May 1646.
Present   Capt Nicholas Martiau   Mr Wm Pryor
                   Mr John Chew   Capt Ralph Wormly
                   Capt John Chisman   Mr Francis Morgan

No.2. p.123   Order that estate of John Abereruniway be appraised by

Edward Michell Thomas Harwood Francis Howard and Richard Dudly. That
Capt John Chisman administer the oath.

No.2. p.123   Order that Thos Jefferyes be Constable for the upper part
of Hampton parish in place of Joseph Torqueniton. Capt Wm Taylor to
admr the oath.

No.2 p.123   That Wm Waters stands indebted to Wm Barker 2 cows with
calves to be paid "at the strawberry banckes or in some convenient
place in hampton River", on 1 May 1645. Waters ordered to pay within
10 days.

No.2. p.123   The dif betw Tho Perrin pltf and John Hammon deft ref by
consent of both parties to Robt Bouth and Kerbery Kiggin to be decided.

No.2. p.123   Upon depositions of Steeven Gill and Baker Cutts, that
Mr Wm Waters owes Francis Flewellen, as by her account, 1000 lb tobo.
Waters ordered to pay.

No.2. p.124   May 25th (1646). Before Capt Nicholas Martiau and Mr
John Chew:
Wm Rennalds confessed judgmt to Mr Wm Pryor for 1073 lb tobo to be pd
at the dwelling house of Mr Pryor according to specialty dated 14th
April 1645, on 10th Sept next.

No.2. p.124   Robt Perry attorney of Richd Milborne confesses judgt
to Charles Smith the assignee of Geo Wescombe for 500 lb tobo "and
one pair of large Ruddr Irons for a shallopp" to be pd within 5 days.

No.2. p.124.   A letter dated 25 May 1646 from Nichos Martiau to Mr
Bouth. Requests that 2 heifers be recorded "the which I have given
unto Geo Beech sonn of George Beech late of Hampton parish late Dec".
If he die before age or marriage the heifers to be returned to the
heirs of Martiau.
Wit: Signed   Nichos Martiau
Wm Barber
John Utye

No.2. p.124   Bill of Sale. 24 May 1646. Arthur Price of York sells
William Davis of "Archers hoope Creek" a cow named "bowleing" with a
calf by her side. Kerbery Kiggin to see sale recorded. A long entry.
Wit: Signed   Arthur Price
Karbery Kiggin
Wm Roberts   (See next entry)

No.2. p.124   Wm Davis assigns whole interest in foregoing bill of sale
to Arthur Price Junior. Karbury Kiggin appointed attorney to see this
recorded.
Wit: Signed   Wm Davis
Karbery Kiggan
Wm Roberts

No.2. p.125   Deed. 25 May 1646. Wm Whitby, gentleman, for personal
considerations, gives over and grants to Richard Lee, 100 acres "on
the North side of Yorke river at the head of tindalls Creek where the
said Lee lived before the Massacre the said land being parte of a
greater Devident purchased by Geo Ludlowe Esqr and me Wm Whitby of
Argoll Yeardly Esqr and is alsoe recorded and this to be a firme alin-
ation which I oblige my selfe my heirs and executors and administrators
to make good against all persons"
Wit: Signature torn away
Wm Brocas
Phillipp Thacker
Ro Bouth Cl Cur
Also an entry, mostly torn away, regarding a survey of this land.
Apparently for Geo Ludlowe and Wm Whitby. The date appears to be 18th
November 1645 but may be 1643.

No.2. p.126   6 April 1646. Wm Todd binds a cow to Wm Pryor as security
for a debt of 707 lb tobo to be pd 10th Nov next at Mr Pryor's house.
Wit: Signed   Wm Todd
Wm Hockaday
John x Hartwell

No.2. p.126   24th Apl 1646. Tho Adams sells Wm Barber and Tho Borne
8 head of cattle.
Wit: Signed   Tho Adams
Henry Lee
Tho Turner
Bond on above. Mutilated. The name Steephen Hamlin appears on the
fragments.

No.2. p.127   25 May 1646. Wm Howard of Hampton parish in York County,
in behalf of his welbeloved wife Ann Howard, relict of George Borne
Junior, deceased, and for divers good causes, gives Thomas Borne, son
of Geo Borne Junior, a heifer, it being of the estate of Borne dec'd.
He to have the heifer when 18 yrs of age and in his minority "my wel-
beloved friends Wm Barber and Elias Richardson to be the overseers of
the said Heifer". If Tho Borne die in minority the heifer to return to
Howard.
Wit: Signed   Wm Howard
Robt Abrall
Phillipp Thacker

No.2. p.127   25th May 1646. Thomas Beale of York sells Tho Shaw a cow.
Wit: Signed   Tho Beale
Phillipp Thacker

No.2. p.127   P of A. 29 March -. Wm Waters to Lewis Burwell to answer
suit of Mr Wm Barker and Mistress Fr: Leuellin.
Wit   Signature torn away
Ro: Vaus
Phillipp Thacker

No.2. p.128   Will of John Abererumway. Dated 4 April 1645. Prob. 25
May 1646.
Goodman Jolly to have 3 cows, a steer in the old field and 2 other
    steers. Also 1/2 of plantation "with the howsing againe that I
    bought of him". All wearing clothes. All hogs.
To Jolly's wife for her sole use a cow and calf bought from Captain
    Chisman. Also 2 cow calves.
To "my Countryman Wm Crumwell" a cow calf.
To Ralph Borer a bed and furniture.
To Goodman Jolly a bed. He to "see me buryed like a man"
Wit:
Nich Pescott   Signed   John Abererunimi
John x funicin
Wm Trumbull

No.2. p.129   Indenture. 10 Sept 1640, Betw Wm Caynehooe of Cheskeack,
clerk, on the one part, and Thos Scarlett on the other part. Caynooe
lets to Scarlett, for 13 years, 50 acres in Chiskeacke parish in the
County of Charles River, adj Utyes Creek and N.W. on the land of John
Dennitt now in possession of Wm Barber. SW and SE into the woods, etc.
As in patent granted said Caynehooe 26 Sept 1639. Scarlett to pay 2
capons yearly.
Wit: Signed   Wm Caynhoo
Tho. Blease

Tho. Scarlett assigns all right in above lease. Does not say who to.
27 Oct 1642
Wit: Signed   Tho x Scarlett
Geo Gill
Rich x Betle

Christopher Deny assigns all right in this lease to Tho. -. 27th -
1643
Wit: Edw Wade   Signature torn away

Tho Hatfield assigns all right in above to Richd Hickes. 24 Aug -.
No witnesses shown.   Signature torn away

No.2. p.130   A Court for Yorke 26 June 1646
Present   Capt Nicholas Martiau   Capt Wm Taylor
               Mr John Chew   Mr Francis Morgan
               Mr Wm Pryor   Mr Row Burnham

No.2. p.130   The estate of Thos Smallcombe "is debtor to Disbursments
as followeth"
                        March 10. 1645/6

                                                              lb tobo
To Thomas Gibson for twoe sheirts   0100
To twoe pr of shooes   0080
To Rondell Renell for twoe barrells of Corne   0300
To twoe gall and a halfe of Sacke bought of Thomas Broughton 0100
To one bottle of drames bought of Thomas Broughton   0025
To Cheese bought of Robert Lewis   0100
To beere sent him in the tyme of his sicknes   0036
To Diett at the ordinary at James Citty   0035
To one blue scarffe   0050
To Diet five monthes at Gibsons   0300
To Tobo pd John Broch as by acct and receipt   0530
To his funerall Charges on steere about 4 yeares old   0700
To one barrell of strong beere   0260
To a Coffin   0150
To two pownd of Powder spent at his funerall   0024
To the minister Clarke and sexton for his buriall   0040
To Thomas Wilkinson as by receipt   0270
To Thomas Taylor as by bill and receipt   0330
To Mr Gill as by bill and receipt   0310
To Robert Taylor as by bill and receipt   0475
To Thomas Broughton as by acco't and receipt   0476
To Thomas Broughton for caske with the tobacco   0030
To William Coxe as by bill and receipt   0090
To Mr John Corker   0161
To John Vaughan as by bill and receipt   0150
To Church warden for parish Dutys   0014
To tob in roule lent him to ●   0020
To John Underwood as by receipt   0030
To Mr Robert Vaus for Mr Thos Vaus by bill and acco't as
     by receipt   1022
To Charges in ● will probate and recording will and
     severall peticons   0300
To Mr Deacon as by receipt   0213

The est of Thomas Smallcombe is credited by contra
By tobacco allowed him by the Assembly for his goeing at
     fort Royall   4000
By twoe Indians sold Sr Wm Berkley   0600

                     (continued)

The estate of Tho Smalloombe (continued)

	lb tobo
By two Indians sold John Hammon	0500
By an Indian sold Capt Thomas Pettus	0600
By Inventory as appeareth	0630
	- - - -
Sume is	6330

June the 26th 1646

Wee finde by Inventory recorded the estate Cr'dt	0630
more by Thomas Gibsons acct	5700
	- - - -
	6330

Estate Debtr by good proffe as bills taken in and	
receipts proveing soe much pd by Tho Gibson	3581
Rests for the Court to have Tho Gibson prove pd	3120

The which was this Day proved by the oath of Thomas Gibson and allowed
by the Court

Teste me   Ro: Bouth   Clr Cur

No.2. p.131   Bill. 24 March 1645/6, Jno Sutton promises to pay Richd
Creedle 500 lb tobo 10 Nov next. Security 2 sows, 12 shoats.
Wit: Signature torn away
Richard Wyate
Anthony Roakeby

No.2. p.132   15 May 1646. Jno Sutton binds a steer for paymt of 500
lb tobo to Giles Tavernor on 15 Oct next.
Wit: Signed   John x Sutton
Hercules Bridges
Robert Wilde

No.2. p.132   19 April 1646. John Sutton sells Hercules Bridges a steer.
The steer was Mr Floyd's and to be ready 2 days before Whitsontide next
Wit: Signed   John x Sutton
Francis Cointard   (?)
17 May 1646. Hercules Bridges assigns his right in the steer to Richd
Watkins
Wit: Signed   Hercules Bridges
Anthony Bassett
Edward x Woodly

1646

No.2. p.133   Bill. 27 March 1646. Luke Davis promises to pay Thomas
Lucas 400 lb tobo 10 Oct next, at the dwelling house of said Davis.
Security, smith's tools, viz, 1 anvil, 1 pr bellows, 1 vice, 1 nail
tool and hammer.
Wit: signed   Luke x Davis
Geo Saughier
Wm Downeman

No.2. p.133   In dif betw Tho Chapman of the new Pawquoson and Abraham
Turner of the same place, concerning title to 450 acres now in the
possession of sd Chapman. An agreement that Chapman give up the land
to Turner upon payment of 9000 lb tobo. This is a long entry. Dated
11 March 1645/6.
Wit: signed   Thomas x Chapman
Thomas Stampe   Abraham Turner
Carbey Kigan

No.2. p.134   P of A. 15 April 1646. John Merryman of the New Pawquo-
son in Va to "welbeloved Frend" John Griggs of the same place to
collect debts in this colony.
Wit: signed   John x Merryman
Humpry Floyd
Mathew Hawkins

No.2. p.135   P of A. 15 April 1646. Christopher Garlington of the New
Pawquoson, planter, to "welbeloved Frend" John Griggs of the same
place to collect debts in Va.
Wit: signed   Christopher x Garlington
Mathew Hawkins
Humpry Floyd

No.2. p.135   Will of Richard Elrington. Dated 26 May 1646. Probated
6 June 1646. Sick in body but in perfect sense.
"unto the poore of St Martins of the feilds" L 10. Sterling "to be
distributed to the severall oldest men as farr as it shall extend at
twoe shillings sixe pence per peece"
To Mistress Margarett and Mistress Mary Pryor L 12, to be pd them or
their supervisors by Mr Ralph Barrett
To "the sd children of Mr Pryor" the produce of a hhd of tobo marked
R.E.W 6.
To Mistress Mary Keton the produce of 3 hhd tobo numbered 3. 4. 5 and
marked as above.
To Ann Claxon servant to Mr Pryor the produce of 1 hhd tobo sent to
Mr Ralph Barrett last year.

(continued)

1646

The Will of Richard Elrington (continued)

To John Flower the produce of 1 hhd tobb, shipped as abovesaid and
what money he can recover "as my due of my Brother"
To Mr Wm Pryor the balance of the estate to and for the use of Mrs
Mary Elrington, he exor.
Wit: Signature torn away
Wm Hockaday
Robert Lee

No. 2. p.136   P of A. 23 May 1646. Wm Gantlett (or Gautlett) to John
Perrin to implead John Clarkson this present Court.
Wit: Signed   Wm Gantlett
Robt Abrall

No. 2. p.136   16th June 1646. Peter Richardson requests Wm Hockaday
to conf a judgt for 1252 lb tobo to Mr Wm Pryor to be pd 10 Nov next.

No. 2. p.136   P of A. 26 April 1646. Edward Shelverdine to "my Freind"
Wm Hockaday to ack a judgt to Mr Pryor for debt of 586 lb tobo.
Wit: Signed   Edward x Shelverdine
Tho Broughton

No. 2. p.136   Inventory of the estate of Thos Broughton deceased 16th
June 1646. Appraised by Nathaniell Warren and John Oliver.
Includes:
a bill of Thomas Kingwell	0100 lb tobo
a bill of Wm Carr	0108
a bill of John Peteetes	0600
a bill of Mr Wm Lights	0300
To tobo recd of Wm Thornton	0350
Due on a/c from Nicholas Jernew	0100
by Order of Court from Edward Grives	0700
50 acres of land with a house	

               Exhibited on oath by Richd Townshend
                     Ro Bouth Clr Cur

No. 2. p.137   Inventory of the estate of John Eaton as appraised by
Edward Peeters and George Beech and sworn to before Mr Hugh Gwln 3
8bor 1645 (3rd Oct 1645). This is a quaint list. It included:
By Sam Seers	300 lb tobo
By John Earle	500
By Anthony Wady	214
By Thomas Floyd	130
By Thomas Sheppard	300

Totals 2702 lb tobo. Exhibited 6 June - by Henry -.

No.2. p.138   Patent. 5 Nov 1639. Sir John Harvey, knt, Governor, etc.,
to Saml Watkins, 250 acres in Charles River Co, in the forest adj land
of John Utye extending from the head of Kings Creek westerly to the
Mayden Swamp and adj land formerly granted the sd Saml Watkins by
patent due by assignment from Joseph Croshaw, for transporting 5
persons.   Signed   John Harvey

No.2. p.138   10 June 1644. Saml Watkins of Queens Creek assigns the
above 250 acres to John Bell. Part of which was due to John Bell by
deed of gift and now the full patent is sold to him.
Wit: Signed   Samuell Watkeses   (sic)
Geo x Clarke
Wm x Roberts

No.2. p.139   1 Oct 1645. John Bell of Queens Creek, planter, assigns
to John Williams the above 250 acres lying in Hampton parish, etc.
Wit: Signed   John Bell
Arthur Price
Tho Deacon

Then follows a further description of this land dated 20 April 1642.
It adjs Bryry Swamp, Wm Taylor's land, Nicholas Comeings, Tho Gibson's
and another dividend of Saml Watkeys (sic). This is signed with a
name appearing to be 'Thomas Smout' which is prob incorrect since part
of it is torn away.

No.2, p.140   Power of Atty. 16 June 1643. John Brooke of Boxked in
the County of Essex (England), Clothyer, to Henry Brooke, Merchant,
Resident in Virginia. To collect debts due him in Virginia "Especially
to recover and secure all such goods wares Debts and things whatsoever
As Barneby Brooke my Brother whoe deceased at Sea goeing to Virginia
aforesaid had in his hands or possession or in Virginia at the tyme
of his Death unto me belonging", etc.
                                            Signed   John Brooke

Sworn before John - notary etc dwelling in the City of London. Date,
signature and witnesses names destroyed.

No.2, p.141   Deed. 14 June 1646. Joseph Croshaw of Hampton parish in
the County of York in Virginia, planter, sells Richard Croshaw, 160
acres, being remainder of a dividend the said Joseph sold to Edward
Adcocke being due by patent dated 29 Oct 1640. The land on N side of
Queens Creek, adjs the Indian field now in possession of sd Joseph
Croshaw.
Wit: Signed   Joseph Croshaw
Ro Bouth

                                1646

No.2. p.141   Bill of Sale. 2 March 1645/6. Henry Brooke of Va, mercht,
sells to Nicholas Heath son of Thos Heath a heifer.
Wit: Signed   Henry Brooke
Nicholas Brooke
Robert Perry

No.2. p.142   Deed of Gift. 25 May 1646. Rich: Pasmuch, for natural
love and affection, gives Edw: Yarborrough Junior a cow calf. The male
increase descending "backe unto me the sd Richard Pasmuch",
Wit: Signed   Rich: R Pasmuch
John Petit surgeon
W Baxter

No.2. p.142   John Griggs attorney to the supervisors of the estate of
Humphry Hanmore, was arrested to answer suit of Wm Whitby who did not
appear to prosecute. Whitby ordered to pay him 50 lb tobo.

No.2. p.142   The dif betw Capt Robt Higginson pltf and John Witherford
to be determined 1st July Court next. Dangerousness of this time will
not permit his leaving his charge and care at Midle plantation for
this Court.

No.2. p.142   Henry Lee arrested to answer suit of Richd James who did
not prosecute. James non suited.

No.2. p.142   By a/c of Henry Lee Admr of John Eaton he having paid to
the assets of the estate to have quietus est.

No.2. p.142   Wm Todd ordered to pay Richd Wells 400 lb tobo in Oct.

No.2. p.143   Wm Grimes arrested at suit of Richd Gonlett, who not
prosecuting is non suited.

No.2. p.143   Dif betw Wm Hockaday assignee of Richard Croshaw pltf
and Joseph Mosely deft referred to 24 July next.

No.2. p.143   Present Mr John Chew

No.2. p.143   Whereas by specialty under the hands of John Scales and
Edward Jorden deceased that they were indebted to George Hopkins decd
500 lb tobo, 1 bbl and 2 bu corn, being due for themselves and their

servants in 1643 for duties and Church levies, order that Mr Wm Pryor admr of Scales and Jorden's estate pay Elizt Hopkins relict and admrx of Geo Hopkins dec'd by 10th November next.

No.2. p.143   Commission of Admr to Capt Nicholas Martiau of the estate of George Beech deceased.

No.2. p.143   Whereas judgt passed agst John Dawson Senior, being security for John Sutton's appearance in January Court to answer suit of Tho Curtis for 1200 lb tobo. Now Dawson producing Sutton, which was accepted by the attorney of Curtis, Sutton is ordered to pay.

No.2. p.143   Wm Gantlett assignee of Tho Doe did implead John Clarkson for 200 lb tobo due by bill. By oath of John Dauson, part of the debt is paid. Doe ordered to allow paymt on a/c of 190 lb tobo.

No.2. p.144   That Francis Beetle owes Thos Bushroode the assignee of Henry Hawley and Matthew Bassett 200 lb tobo. Beetle ordered to pay. "and alsoe that the non suite obteyned by misinformation of the said Beetle in January Court last against the said Bushroode be voyd".

No.2. p.144   Ann Snoden an orphan now in keeping of Capt Nicholas Martiau, "haveing noe meanes at all left her towards her mentaynnance being now about the age of seaven yeares", is bound to Capt Martiau for 9 years from this date. Capt Martiau "according to his own proffer to give the said Ann Snoden forthwith a cowe calfe of three mounthes old and to keepe the said calfe with all her female increase for the for the said Ann Snoden during the tyme of her apprentishipp and to give an yearely ac'ot thereof to this Court". Capt Wm Taylor to see the calf marked.

No.2. p.144   Thos Beale owing Hercules Bridges 380 lb tobo "for the attendance of himselfe and certeyne men at his charge on Mistress Mary Wormeley when shee was under arrest by vertue of an order of Court from the Governour and Counsell directed to the said Mr Beale for that purpose". Beale ordered to pay.

No.2. p.144   Abraham Cayne owing Hercules Bridges 438 lb tobo by a/c, Thos Beale admr of Cayne's estate ordered to pay.

No.2. p.144   Daniel Holland owing the estate of Humphry Hanmore 522 lb tobo is ordered to pay by 10 Nov next.

1646

No.2. p.145   Whereas Humphrey Hanmore did, in his will, give Daniel
Holland one year of his time, the supervisors of the estate ordered to
do so.

No.2. p.145   That Humphry Hanmore by will gave Eliz Coole and Francis
Coole the children of Francis Coole a cow calf "the first that fell
after his Decease", and also a sow to the wife of said Francis Coole,
the supervisors of the estate ordered to pay the legacies.

No.2. p.145   That Humphry Hanmore by will gave to Geo Haderell "soe
much cloath as would make him a suite of clothes". Supervisors of the
estate ordered to pay this legacy.

No.2. p.145   That Steeven Gill obtained an attachmt agst the estate
of Henry Pountnell for 600 lb tobo in July last Court, which the Sheriff executed upon 350 lb tobo in hands of Hugh Dowdy and 5 shoats in
the hands of Joane Trotter.

No.2. p.145   Order that the land and plantation belonging to Leift
Nicholas Steelwill on West Creek be rented out. The rent to go to
creditors. If he comes again the land to be returned to him.

No.2. p.146   Nicholas Brooke Jr owing Tho Broughton assignee of John
Clieverius 20 shillings Sterling. order that the debt be paid.

No.2. p.146   Nicholas Brooke arrested at suit of Bicholas Sebrill
who did not appear. Sebrill non suited.

No.2. p.146   By a/c of Tho Gibson admr of est of Tho Smalocombe, he
having pd out the whole estateby inventory to have quietus est.

No.2. p.146   There is due Mr John Chew 696 lb tobo "from tytieular
men in Yorke parish for his charges expended in the tyme of being
Burgesse for the said parish", which tobacco should have been collected
by the last year's sheriff but no payment made. Order that the tobo
be raised at the next levy for the parish of York.

No.2. p.146   Order that certificate be granted Mr Wm Pryor for 200
acres for transporting "of fower Negroes", viz Peeter, John, Grace
and Kathren.

1646

No.2. p.146   Order that Richd Vaugon be appointed constable in place of Christopher Stookes. Oath to be admr by Capt Jno Chisman.

No.2. p.146   That Humphry Hanmer dec'd was indebted to Rd Belchamber by a/c 509 lb tobo. Order for paymt.

No.2. p.146   That Humphry Hanmore by will gave Rd Belchamber 1 hhd tobo. The supervisors of the estate ordered to pay.

No.2. p.147   David Doehart arrested to answer suit of Geo Ludlowe is ordered to pay debt of 200 lb tobo.

No.2. p.147   Fif betw Mr Hugh Gwin pltf and Denis Steevens, Jno Smith, Leift Tho Dobbs and Jno Dyer defts to next (July) Court.

No.2. p.147   Court Order that John Hansford and Robt Lewis for Hampton parish, Samuell Sallis and Jeffery Power for York parish and Edward Michell and Abraham Turner for Pawquoson parish take a perfect list of the tytheables in the several parishes. As also of all cows of 3 years old, horses, mares and geldings of 3 yrs old and upwards, sheep and goats. And to deliver the lists to the Sheriff by 25th of this present June. "and that every mans name be taken particularly".

No.2. p.147   That the sheriff arrested Nicholas Jurneur, Wm Sawyer, Martin Westerlincke, John Perrin and John Thomas. All to answer suit of Richd Malborne who did not appear against them. Malborne is non suited and ordered to pay 50 lb tobo to each.

No.2. p.147   June 16th 1646
Judgements confessed before Capt Martiau and Mr John Chew
Peter Richardson to Mr Wm Pryor 1200 lb tobo.
John Mallor to James Stooke 337 lb tobo.

(the end)

The next Court for York 24 July 1646.

INDEX

Plunckett, Edmund 20
Pollin possibly as Pilling.
Poopeley, - , 62
        Capt Richd. 60. 61
Poore, Jeffry 48
Popeley, Mrs. 78
        Eliz: 81
        Capt Richd 64
Popley, Eliz: 40
Pountnell, Hen: 93
Power, Jeffery 46. 75. 94
Pownsey, Jno. 47
Poyethres, Lt. Fr: 81
Poynter, Jno. 61
        Thos. 45
Pratt, Jno. 38
Preston, Joseph 53
Price, - , 48
        Arthur 21. 42. 43. 45
          46. 57. 77. 79. 83.
          90.
        Arthur Jr. 84
        Howell 77
Pryor, Margaret and Mary daus
    of Mr. Wm Pryor   88
Pryor, William 7. 16. 29. 30
    33. 35. 40. 41. 47. 49. 53
    55. 56. 64. 73. 74. 76. 77
    78. 83. 84. 88. 89. 92. 93
    94
Pryor, Wm as Justice. 10. 11.
    13. 14. 15. 16. 17. 18. 19
    21. 23. 24. 25. 26. 28. 31
    46. 48. 82. 86
Pucoke, Hen: 81

Quoke, Wm. 74

Rainson, Peeter 81
Ramsey, Thos. 20. 30. 39. 43
          59. 63
Records - that some were lost
      54
Reddley, Peeter 45
Rennalds, Wm. 83
Renell, Rondell 86
Reynalds, Tho. 38
        Wm. 19. 20. 21. 26

Richardson, - , 50
        Elias 63. 84
        Peter 55. 89. 94
Rideell, Geo. 42
Ridley see Reddley
Rigby, Peter 25
Roahds, Tho. 38
Roakeby, Antho: 87
Robbertts, Wm 26
Roberts, Edw. 58. 70
        Wm. 69. 83. 84. 90
Robinson, Jno. 57
Robison, Jno. 42
Rogers, Jas. 49
Roggers, Jeremiah 24
Rooe, Michell 50
Rookes, Hugh 59
Rose, Jno. 44
Row (?),Rice 57
Rowlston, - , 27
        Lyonell 14. 15
        Lyonell as Justice 5. 6
Russell, Richd 21
Ruttland, Geo. 39

St Martins in the Fields, London.
    88
Sadler, Roger 41. 42
Saker, John Jr and Sr   38. 43
Sallis, Saml 94
Sanderson, Isack 38
Saturwight, Michael 29. 46
Satturthwaite, Nich: 66
    (The above 2 may be the same
    person under either name. The
    original record being very
    difficult in the entries. B.F.
Saughier, Geo. 66. 68. 88
Savage, - , 78
Sawyer, Wm. 43. 63. 79. 94
Saxe, Tho. 61. 75
Sayle, Humph: 79
Scales, Jno. 21. 55. 91. 92
Scarlett, Tho. 85
Sebriell, Nicho. 57. 61. 93
Seers, Sam 89
Sewell, Mr. 40
Seawell, Arthur 71. 80. Arthur
    and his wife 55.

Yarborrough, Edw Jr. 91
Yarrow, Edw Jr and Sr 66
Yeardley, Argoll 84
Youile possibly here as Whowell. Yes I
      Think this must be Ewell, or as you
      please.   B.F.
Young, Mr.   12